ADVENTURE GAMES BOOK

The Hidden Blueprints Game

based on Capt. W. E. Johns'
Biggles in the Blue

Illustrated by Gary Rees

GW01057412

HODDER AND STOUGHTON
LONDON SYDNEY AUCKLAND TORONTO

British Library Cataloguing in Publication Data

The hidden blueprints game
  I. Rees, Gary   II. Johns, W. E. (William Earl), *1893–1968.*
  Biggles in the blue   III. Series
  823′.914 [J]

  ISBN 0-340-50119-7

First published 1989
Second impression 1994

Published by Hodder and Stoughton Children's Books,
a division of Hodder Headline Plc.
338 Euston Road, London NW1 3BH

Photoset by Rowland Phototypesetting Ltd,
Bury St Edmunds, Suffolk

Printed in Great Britain by
Cox & Wyman Ltd, Reading, Berkshire

You have often read about Biggles' air investigations . . . now here's your chance to take part in one!

This time YOU are in charge. YOU have to fly the aircraft, navigate the course, read the maps. Whether Biggles and his team solve the case is in your hands.

You will not necessarily solve the case on your first attempt. It may well take several goes. Keep trying, though, and you will eventually be successful.

Even when you have solved the mystery, the game can still be played again. For there are many different routes to the solution – and each route involves different clues and adventures.

So the game can be played over and over. As many times as you like!

HOW TO PLAY

To solve the case, you have to go with Biggles and his team on a flying mission through the book. You do this by starting at PARAGRAPH ONE and then following the instructions to other paragraphs.

Many of the paragraphs will ask you to work out some sort of problem or clue. You do not have to work out every one of these to solve the overall case . . . but the more you manage the more successful you're likely to be. The fewer problems/clues you crack, the less chance you have of completing the mission.

To help you work out the problems/clues, there are several pieces of equipment available – a compass, a map, a pair of binoculars and a codebook. You can start with only one of these EQUIPMENT CARDS but you will often pick up others as the game goes along. Occasionally, however, you will be asked to give some up as well.

To hold your EQUIPMENT CARDS during the mission, there is an AIRCRAFT CARD. This will tell you exactly which EQUIPMENT CARDS you have for use at any one time (so, after they've helped in solving a particular problem/clue, always remember to return them to your AIRCRAFT CARD!). Any EQUIPMENT CARDS not in your AIRCRAFT CARD **cannot be used or consulted** – and therefore should be kept out of play.

Of course, no flying mission could possibly take place without fuel. You are therefore also given a FUEL GAUGE. The position of the pointer on the gauge shows you how much fuel you have at any particular time during the mission.

If a paragraph informs you that Biggles' aircraft has consumed or lost a quantity of fuel, then you must move the pointer on the gauge one coloured segment **clockwise**. For example, if the pointer is currently on *ample*, it should be turned to *low*.

When you have to move the pointer into the *danger* segment, it means there is not enough fuel to continue the mission and it must immediately be aborted. In other words, the game is over and you will have to start again from **paragraph one**. (You might like to set off with a different EQUIPMENT CARD this time to see if it gives you any more luck.)

READY TO START

An experienced fighter-pilot, 'BIGGLES' (real name James Bigglesworth) now works for New Scotland Yard. He is in charge of a small *air police investigation team*. This was set up to deal with those special cases that are outside the scope of normal ground-based staff. The other members of this very select team are BERTIE (a monocled eccentric, used to the good things in life), GINGER (a very intelligent – if rather young – pilot) . . . and a vintage light aircraft! Although he has often been offered a more modern machine, Biggles still trusts his beloved Auster four-seater.

News has just reached Biggles' superior, Air Commodore Raymond, that a certain Werner Wolff has died. Wolff used to work for an enemy intelligence service but then suddenly disappeared . . . taking with him the only blueprints of a new nuclear missile! At that time it was thought that he intended to sell these to the highest bidder.

It turns out that Wolff had been living in Jamaica under an alias. This is revealed when the Jamaican authorities search a dead man's house and find Wolff's original passport tucked away in the safe! Unfortunately, however, the search does not uncover the missing blueprints. It is essential that these blueprints are found quickly as the enemy intelligence service would obviously be making every effort to get them back!

The only possible clues Wolff left as to the whereabouts of the blueprints were a notebook containing various codes and a strange photograph he had taken. It was of a flamingo standing in a marsh! Could this be his little joke; a reference to Flamingo Island – a large, sparsely populated landmass some fifty miles west of Jamaica?

Well, it is the only lead they have, so Biggles and his team are ordered over to Flamingo Island. They must find and destroy the blueprints before they fall into the wrong hands . . .

To join the team on this mission, you will first of all need to prepare your aircraft. So pick out the AIRCRAFT CARD and keep it near you. You must now choose a piece of equipment to take with you. Biggles and his team each have a map, a compass, a pair of binoculars and a photocopy of Wolff's codebook – but you can start with only *one* of these. Which do you think would be the most useful? Insert the EQUIPMENT CARD you have chosen into the slit of your AIRCRAFT CARD and keep the remaining three EQUIPMENT CARDS out of play until told you can pick them up.

Now for the FUEL GAUGE. You start off with a full tank, so turn the pointer to the *full* segment. Don't forget that during the mission, however, you may sometimes be instructed to move the pointer to a lower reading – and you must comply with this.

Remember: When the pointer reaches the DANGER segment, the mission has to stop and you must start the game all over again.

Just over two weeks later, the Auster was cruising in a perfect Caribbean sky. Biggles was sitting at the front left of the plane operating the controls, Bertie was to his right and Ginger was behind them both – excitedly leaning between them every so often! Their plane had been transported to Jamaica by a Royal Navy aircraft-carrier. During this voyage, floats had been fitted to the Auster's undercarriage to convert it to a seaplane. It was thought that Flamingo Island was likely to offer more water to land on than suitable ground! 'Flamingo Island should be coming into view very soon now, shouldn't it?' Ginger asked eagerly as he surveyed the blue-green sea below. 'It must be near on forty miles we've clocked up since Jamaica.' Glancing at the milometer, Biggles told him that they had actually flown *forty-two* miles. 'So you're right, Ginger,' he added, starting to search the horizon himself, 'Flamingo Island should be appearing any moment now!'

Throw the SPECIAL DICE to determine which of the three is to spot Flamingo Island first.

        BIGGLES thrown   go to 226
        BERTIE thrown   go to 53
        GINGER thrown   go to 127

2

As Ginger was studying his compass, Bertie suddenly thumped his head. 'What a numbskull I am!' he declared. 'A complete and utter one! Of course those rocks couldn't have been arranged by Wolff! Look at the size of them. Ten men couldn't lift one of those – let alone just Wolff. Obviously they're in that arrow pattern by mere chance!' As Biggles now left the bottle-shaped isle behind them, heading towards Flamingo Island itself, he gave the fuel gauge a quick check. That fifty-mile flight from Jamaica meant that it was a quarter down already!

Move the pointer on your FUEL GAUGE one coloured segment clockwise. Now go to 215.

3

'Hey, hang on a second, old boy!' Bertie said, stopping Ginger as he reached into his pocket for his compass. '*Any* palm-tree would look like an arrow if it were on its side. You need more evidence than that!' But Ginger said that there *was* more evidence. 'Look at the break in the trunk,' he insisted. 'It's surely much too clean to have been caused by the wind!' *Go to 128.*

4

The Auster now started to fly *across* the island, passing over the palm-trees that fringed its coastline. Ginger noticed how bent their trunks were, the result of the strong winds that often occurred in the

Caribbean. He decided to find out the direction of the prevailing wind. It could be quite useful to them. All he had to do was check on his compass which direction the palms were leaning!

Use your COMPASS CARD to find the direction the palms are leaning yourself by placing it exactly over the shape below – and with the pointer touching north. Then go to the number that appears in the window. If you don't have a COMPASS CARD, you'll have to guess which of the numbers to go to.

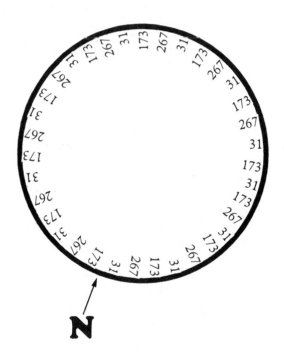

'I'm afraid our Mr Wolff's a bit of a joker!' Bertie remarked irritably as he consulted his codebook. 'Those symbols are meaningless – at least, none of them appears in his codebook. I think the dear fellow was just having us on!' Ginger was even less amused, huffily screwing up the piece of paper he had so eagerly scribbled the symbols on and throwing it out of the window. It was only then that he realised they were drawn on the back of his map! 'Wolff's spirit must be having a good old laugh at us,' he commented sourly.

If you have it there, remove the MAP from your AIRCRAFT CARD. Now go to 218.

6

Before Ginger had a chance to study his map, though, Biggles had swooped down, right over the lagoon. 'It looks pretty deep to me!' Bertie said as they rose up into the air again. 'I'm sure we can chance a landing.' So Biggles immediately turned the plane round again, banking sharply to the right. He then gently landed it on the lagoon, aiming as near to one end as he dared. They were still afloat! Just before switching off the engine, Biggles checked the plane's fuel gauge. The pointer had dropped quite a bit since he'd last looked.

Move the pointer on your FUEL GAUGE one coloured segment clockwise. Now go to 160.

Ginger deciphered the coded message as: *THESE NEGATIVES WERE FOUND IN WOLFF'S HOUSE – THEY MIGHT BE SOME SORT OF CLUE*. For a while none of them could speak. 'Well, it's obvious we're not the only ones who are searching for those blueprints,' Biggles commented at last. 'Nor are we the only ones who think they might be on this island!' With considerable anxiety the trio climbed into their plane, ready to take off again. *Go to 162.*

'How about near that clump of palm-trees on the river's right bank?' Ginger suggested. 'They'll give us a mooring for the plane.' So Biggles banked the Auster towards the palm-trees, gently pushing on its control column. As they descended, Ginger reached into his jacket pocket for his map so he could look for the marsh. He wanted to know exactly what size it was.

Use your MAP to find which square the flamingo marsh is in – then follow the instruction. If you don't have a MAP in your AIRCRAFT CARD, you'll have to guess which instruction to follow.

If you think D3	go to 270
If you think C3	go to 37
If you think B3	go to 164

9

'I'd rather explore the marsh first, if you don't mind,' Biggles told Bertie as he was taking out his copy of the codebook. 'I don't think we have many hours of light left and we really must give that priority. We'll take the camera with us and have another look at it later.' They were a good half mile further on their trek towards the marsh when Biggles realised his compass was no longer in his pocket. It must have slipped out when he had tripped over the camera!

If you have it there, remove the COMPASS CARD from your AIRCRAFT CARD. Now go to 50.

10

'By Jove, listen to this!' Bertie exclaimed when he had used his copy of Wolff's codebook to make sense of the symbols on the cigarette case. *'THE THIRD CIGARETTE FROM THE RIGHT CONTAINS A DEADLY POISON.* What a charming message! You know, our friend Wolff sounds a really nasty piece of work. Presumably he intended to offer that lethal cigarette to anyone who tried to arrest him!' Bertie was just tossing the offending cigarette out of his window, into the sea below, when Ginger gave an excited cry. 'There's the shipwreck!' he exclaimed, pointing ahead. *Go to 186.*

Bertie reached the hut first, sure that it could provide the vital clue they were looking for. No sooner had he stepped inside the cane and palm-leaf structure – so flimsy that it looked about to fall down at any moment! – than he started to search the mud floor for anything that Wolff might have dropped. 'Look at this, old chaps!' he said delightedly as the others arrived. 'It's one of those foil-backed packets that films come in. And there appears to be a coded message scribbled on the outside. I'll see if the symbols are the same as in Wolff's codebook!'

Use your CODEBOOK CARD to find out what the symbols mean by decoding the instruction below. If you don't have a CODEBOOK CARD in your AIRCRAFT CARD, go to 126 instead.

'Look, there's a harbour down there!' Bertie said, after they had flown right up the east coast of the island. 'It looks rather derelict, but nevertheless suitable for landing. We shouldn't have any worries about hidden rocks or the water not being deep enough, anyway.' So Biggles pushed down on the control column until the Auster was skimming the water at the entrance to the harbour. He then carefully steered the plane in, bringing it to a stop alongside one of the rickety wooden piers. *Go to 100.*

13

After a quarter of an hour of sharp banks and turns, zig-zagging this way and that, Biggles quietened the Auster's engine again. 'No, I don't hear her!' he said, keenly listening at his opened window. 'Either the plane was totally innocent – or it worked out what I was up to and held back. Let's just hope it was the former!' As Biggles made for the shore of Flamingo Island once more, he glanced at the fuel gauge. That merry dance had cost them – the pointer had dropped quite a bit!

Move the pointer on your FUEL GAUGE one coloured segment clockwise. Now go to 228.

14

'It's fake all right!' Bertie said as he reached the flamingo, giving it a tap. 'Listen, it's hollow. Our friend Wolff certainly liked his little jokes, didn't he? I assume it was he who stuck it here.' This assumption seemed to be confirmed when Ginger discovered a message written on the underside of the plastic replica. It read: *WALK SEVENTY PACES DUE SOUTH*. He eagerly took out his compass!

Use your COMPASS CARD to find due south yourself by placing it exactly over the shape below – and with the pointer touching north. Then go to the number that appears in the window. If you don't have a COMPASS CARD, you'll have to guess which of the numbers to go to.

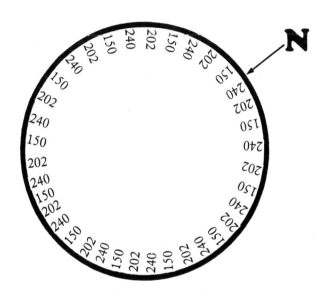

'The island's north-west of us,' Ginger told Biggles when he had found its direction on his compass. It was a good job they had taken this precaution because the haze soon swallowed up the purplish hump once more! 'North-west, you say?' Biggles checked as he pressed down on his left rudder pedal to point the plane in that direction. 'I wonder how long it will be before the island appears again.' The answer was ten minutes – and this time it was considerably larger! Another couple of miles and they should reach it . . . *Go to 256.*

16

When Bertie was ready with his codebook, however, he saw that it had all been wishful thinking. Now that the buoy was more stable, the 'coded message' proved to be no more than simple scratch marks! The calmer water revealed another disappointment: they could now see right down to the sea bed . . . and the only thing beneath the buoy was a huge slab of concrete! Certainly no blueprints in a bottle! 'I knew the possibility of finding them this early was just too good to be true,' Bertie said disappointedly as the Auster skated up into the air again. *Go to 45.*

17

'I don't know about a life-jacket,' Bertie said thoughtfully as they now flew over the island's shore, 'but I think I *have* spotted something! Can you see that statue of an admiral down there? Isn't it rather odd? Look, his telescope's pointing not out to sea, as shown on the map, but inland!' The others agreed it was somewhat unusual but they failed to see what it had to do with Wolff. 'Perhaps it was *him* who turned it that way!' Bertie explained with growing excitement, 'to show which direction to travel across the island for the blueprints! I'm going to get out my compass.'

Use your COMPASS CARD to find the direction the statue is indicating by placing it exactly over the shape below – and with the pointer touching north. Then go to the number that appears in the window. If you don't have a COMPASS CARD, you'll have to guess which of the numbers to go to.

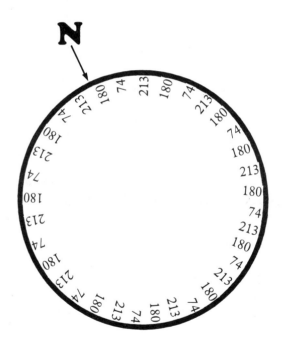

18

Ginger's map not only showed the position of the statue but it also told whom it commemorated. One Sir James Wetherby – first governor on the island! As Ginger was folding up his map again, a pair of binoculars slid out from under his seat. Since they didn't belong to any of them, he could only assume that they had been dropped by a passenger on one of their previous missions!

If you don't already have it there, put the BINOCULARS CARD into your AIRCRAFT CARD. Now go to 173.

19

'It looks as if I was wrong about Wolff being behind this coded message,' Biggles said disappointedly when he had consulted his codebook. 'At any rate, none of these symbols appear in this book of his. Either he was using another code that we don't know about or, probably more likely, the message was carved by someone completely different!' Nevertheless, the trio made a quick search round the top of the mountain – just in case. 'Not a sausage!' Bertie remarked wearily half an hour or so later. 'Come on – we might as well start the long walk down again!' *Go to 263.*

'Do you speak English?' Biggles asked the old man gently as they stepped inside his hut. 'We'd like to know if you ever encountered a man with round glasses and a blond moustache in this area? It's very important to us.' The old man continued to puff at his pipe for a while and then rose slowly to his feet and went out of the hut. He pointed a withered arm into the distance. 'I wonder if that's to tell us the direction Wolff went when he left the village?' Biggles asked bewilderedly. 'I'll check which way he's pointing on my compass.'

Use your COMPASS CARD to find the direction the old man is indicating by placing it exactly over the shape below – and with the pointer touching north. Then go to the number that appears in the window. If you don't have a COMPASS CARD, you'll have to guess which of the numbers to go to.

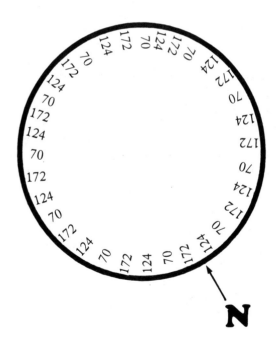

Ginger's map showed that the jagged rocks were in the far north-west of the island. 'That means that we have now flown right across it,' he told the others. 'From opposite corner to opposite corner!' So Biggles turned the Auster eastwards, deciding to fly the other diagonal across the island. *Go to 71.*

The plane was soon circling over the marsh and Biggles wondered if it were deep enough for them to land on. 'I wouldn't risk it if I were you, old boy,' Bertie advised him. 'Look, even in the very centre of the marsh there are reeds growing. So it can't be that deep!' Fortunately, the marsh was very close to the island's one river and Biggles decided to alight there instead. 'I'll follow the river until it becomes a little wider, though,' he told them, turning the Auster seawards. 'There's no point in making it difficult for ourselves!' *Go to 41.*

'You're pointing north-west,' Biggles explained to the fascinated boy, letting him watch the needle gradually settle as he held the compass on the palm on his hand. 'So all we have to do is fly north-west in our plane and then we should find the shipwreck. Many thanks for your help once again!' As Biggles returned to the Auster, wading through the marshy water, he suddenly felt something catch his right foot. He put his hand into the water and fished out a looped leather strap – a strap that was attached to a small case. Inside the case, and surprisingly dry, was a pair of binoculars. Biggles wondered if they might have been Wolff's!

If you don't already have it there, put the BINOCULARS CARD into your AIRCRAFT CARD. Now go to 221.

Bertie was still removing his binoculars from their case, however, when Ginger suddenly spotted the waterfall ahead of them. It was almost lost in the dense vegetation but they could see its spray steaming up above the trees. It was obviously quite a powerful one! As Biggles turned the Auster towards the waterfall, he glanced down at his instrument panel to check the plane's fuel situation. It was lower than he'd hoped!

Move the pointer on your FUEL GAUGE one coloured

*segment clockwise. **Now go to 153.*** (Remember: when the pointer reaches the DANGER segment on your FUEL GAUGE, you must immediately stop the game and start all over again from the beginning.)

25

As soon as Ginger had found south-east on his compass, they started following that direction, wondering how far they were meant to go. They found themselves skirting the edge of the marsh, towards the spot where a solitary flamingo stood amongst the reeds. They expected it to fly off at any moment but it appeared entirely unconcerned by their approach. Bertie suddenly realised why. 'By Jove, that's not a flamingo at all!' he exclaimed. 'At least, not a real one. It's just a plastic replica!' **Go to 14.**

'We didn't mean to scare your flamingos,' Biggles apologised to the woman. 'It's just that our business here is very important. Please, tell us about this other man.' The woman took a while to respond, but eventually she seemed to feel that Biggles was a person she could trust. 'The man took some photographs here,' she explained. 'But I could tell he wasn't a real bird-lover. I knew he was up to no good . . . so I secretly followed him. He walked many miles – to the large waterfall. Then he hid behind it!' The trio all wanted to ask the woman exactly the same question. It was just a matter of who was going to be the quickest with it!

*Throw the **SPECIAL DICE** to decide.*

BIGGLES thrown	go to 175
BERTIE thrown	go to 247
GINGER thrown	go to 134

The team had just counted their tenth pace eastwards from the chiselled message, emerging at one side of the waterfall, when the rock face just above Biggles' head suddenly exploded into tiny splinters. 'What on earth was . . .?' he began, just as the rock splintered again, and then a third time. They were being fired at! 'The gunman must be hiding somewhere in those trees,' Biggles said breathlessly as they all made a run for it. 'In fact, I'd say there're at least three of them!' They hoped to lose the gunmen so they could return to the waterfall but they found themselves being driven back towards their plane. 'We'll have to leave the island and the blueprints for the time being!' Biggles decided reluctantly as they all quickly hauled themselves into the Auster. 'We'll only come back when we've got some weapons of our own!'

Your mission wasn't successful, unfortunately. If you would like another attempt at it, you must start the game all over again from the beginning. Try setting off with a different EQUIPMENT CARD this time to see if it gives you any more luck!

28

'Ah, so *that's* why you sped off so guiltily!' Bertie chuckled as he stared down at the boy sprawled out on the ground, noticing the bright yellow mess all over his front. 'You were stealing the flamingo's eggs!' He helped the boy to his feet. 'Now I promise not to inform anyone about this,' he told him with a friendly wink, 'if you help us with our very important mission. All I want to know is, did you ever see a man taking photographs on this marsh, quite some time ago?' The boy didn't answer for a while but then, just as Biggles and Ginger arrived, he nodded his head. 'Yes, I did,' he said. 'He was a European man, like yourself!' *Go to 154.*

'I know it probably sounds like wishful thinking, old chaps,' Bertie remarked not long after, 'but I think I *might* just have found something! Look at those rocks down there on that beach. Am I just being fanciful, or do they seem to be in the shape of an arrow?' Glancing at the beach themselves, Biggles and Ginger immediately saw what Bertie meant. The pattern of the rocks *did* very much suggest an arrow! Could it be that they had been arranged there by Wolff to denote which direction one should fly across Flamingo Island for the blueprints? Ginger started searching his pockets for a compass!

Use your COMPASS CARD to find the direction the rocks are indicating by placing it exactly over the shape below – and with the pointer touching north. Then go to the number that appears in the window. If you don't have a COMPASS CARD, you'll have to guess which of the numbers to go to.

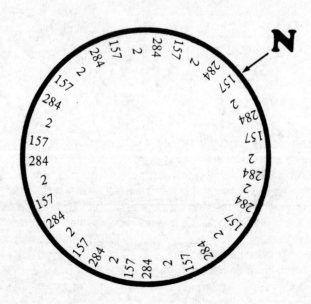

Bertie's map showed that the bay with the sand-dunes was about halfway up the *east* side of the island. 'Well, how does the bay look for a landing, old chap?' he asked Biggles as he folded up his map again. 'Are you going to risk it?' Biggles made one last check for any treacherous green patches. He was confident there weren't any. 'Yes!' he replied, preparing for the descent. ***Go to 190.***

But by the time Ginger had found which pocket his compass was in, the palms had grown considerably more dense. As a result, they leaned far less – if at all! And Ginger felt his heart sink as he stared down at the thickening vegetation. Trying to find the blueprints in that jungle was going to be virtually impossible! They'd flown a few more miles when Biggles felt his heart begin to sink too. For he had checked the fuel gauge and noticed that the pointer had dropped quite a bit since he'd last looked. At this rate, they wouldn't have enough juice to do a decent search of the island!

Move the pointer on your FUEL GAUGE one coloured segment clockwise. Now go to 173.

32

'The arrow's pointing north-west,' Ginger said when he had checked its direction on his compass. 'North-west must be the direction we're meant to fly in then,' he added fervently. 'It must be!' As the Auster now began its journey across the island – a monotonous carpet of dark green vegetation – Bertie suddenly noticed a folded sheet of paper near his feet. 'Well, I'll be blowed!' he remarked as he opened out the sheet. 'It's another copy of Wolff's codebook! How on earth did that get here?' Of course, there was *one* way. Someone must have been snooping round their plane before it had left Jamaica and the codebook must have dropped out of their pocket. But surely no one else had a copy of Wolff's codebook?

If you don't already have it there, put the CODEBOOK CARD into your AIRCRAFT CARD. Now go to 269.

33

'It looks awfully like the place has been abandoned,' Bertie said as the trio now approached the village. 'There's not a soul in sight!' A quick walk round the straw-roofed huts confirmed Bertie's fears. The village obviously hadn't been inhabited for quite some time. As they were returning, rather disappointed, to their plane at the beach, Biggles stopped to look for the village on his map. It would at least show them exactly where they were on the island!

Use your MAP to find which square the village is in – then follow the instruction. **If you don't have a MAP in your AIRCRAFT CARD, you'll have to guess which instruction to follow.**

If you think B1   go to 193
If you think B2   go to 106
If you think C1   go to 58

34

As Bertie was removing his binoculars from their case, however, Biggles gently twisted his friend's head towards the left. He chuckled as he did so. 'By gosh, there are *two* lakes down there!' Bertie said, rather embarrassed. 'Our plane is at the end of the other one!' They now started the long descent towards the plane, reaching it just under an hour later. As Biggles warmed the engine ready to take off again, he glanced at the fuel gauge. The pointer was lower than he was expecting!

Move the pointer on your FUEL GAUGE one coloured segment clockwise. Now go to 162.

'*THIS – IS – THE – PROPERTY – OF – WERNER – WOLFF*,' Biggles read out slowly, using his codebook to decode the symbols on the rucksack. He allowed himself a little satisfied smile. Wolff certainly seemed to enjoy his secrecy! As they were about to return to their plane, Ginger found further proof that Wolff had been in this area. For glinting in the grass was a small compass. And etched on the back were the initials *W.W.*!

If you don't already have it there, put the COMPASS CARD into your AIRCRAFT CARD. Now go to 71.

'If the marsh is quite large,' Ginger said after thinking about it for a while, 'it might be shown on our maps. It wouldn't do any harm to look anyway!' So he immediately reached into his inside jacket pocket for his map . . .

Use your MAP to find which square the marsh with the flamingos is in – then follow the instruction. If you don't have a MAP in your AIRCRAFT CARD, you'll have to guess which instruction to follow.

If you think B3	go to 219
If you think D3	go to 155
If you think C3	go to 49

Studying his map, Ginger worked out the area of the marsh to be about four square miles. So searching it for clues was going to take a considerable amount of time! He folded up his map again as the Auster skated along the river's surface. It sprayed to a halt only metres from where Ginger had suggested: parallel to the clump of palm-trees. It was another perfect touch-down from Biggles! *Go to 164.*

Bertie was just about to consult his copy of Wolff's codebook to see if it contained the same symbols when Ginger spotted the shipwreck. It was about a mile ahead of them, a few hundred metres out to sea. 'Well, let's hope this is the end of our search!' Biggles remarked as he glanced at his fuel gauge. 'Our juice is a lot lower than I thought!'

Move the pointer on your FUEL GAUGE one coloured segment clockwise. Now go to 186. (Remember: when the pointer reaches the DANGER segment on your FUEL GAUGE, you must immediately stop the game and start all over again from the beginning.)

Ginger reached the hut first, although the others arrived only a minute or so later. 'Looks as if it's about to fall down!' Biggles commented as he and Bertie joined Ginger inside the small, palm-leaf structure. 'Have you found anything interesting yet, Ginger?' As a matter of fact, Ginger *had*. It was a faded note pinned to one of the hut's supporting bamboos! 'It says: *WALK SOUTH-EAST OF THE HUT,*' Ginger announced, excitedly reaching into his jacket pocket for his compass.

Use your COMPASS CARD to find south-east yourself by placing it exactly over the shape below – and with the pointer touching north. Then go to the number that appears in the window. If you don't have a COMPASS CARD, you'll have to guess which of the numbers to go to.

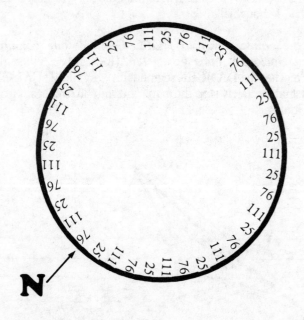

As Ginger was unfolding his map, Biggles had a longer look at this large derelict house, wondering what it was. He noticed that there was a tall flagpole in front of it. So he guessed that it was once some sort of government building – maybe from the island's colonial days. *Go to 272.*

'Right, it's more than wide enough here,' Biggles said about two miles further down as the river started to broaden out into the sea. 'There doesn't seem to be too much silting there either. Anyone like to suggest the exact part I should aim for?'

Throw the SPECIAL DICE to decide who is to make the suggestion.

BIGGLES thrown	go to 60
BERTIE thrown	go to 184
GINGER thrown	go to 8

'It says: *THE BLUEPRINTS ARE HIDDEN IN THE SCHOONER'S FIGUREHEAD!*' Bertie told the others ec-statically as he decoded the message carved into the mast. They all hurried to the very front of the ship and Bertie stretched his arm underneath the prow. 'It's a mermaid's head by the feel of it,' he said tensely as he passed his fingers over the wooden sculpture. 'Now what do we have here, stuffed in the old girl's mouth? It feels like a plastic tube.' Pulling the object out with a firm yank, he saw that his guess was exactly right. It was a plastic tube . . . and tightly rolled up inside were the blueprints! 'Well done, team!' Biggles exclaimed proudly.

And well done to YOU too. You have successfully completed the mission!

43

'I'm afraid it's two of us imagining things now, Bertie!' Biggles told his friend before he was ready with his binoculars. '*I* can see the island as well!' Bertie kept his binoculars in his lap for a moment and then opened his window to have another stare at the horizon. 'By Jove, you're right!' he exclaimed, shielding his eyes with his map. 'There *is* some land there. Unless all three of us are imagining things, of course!' Bertie was just lowering the map from his eyes when the plane was suddenly jerked by a gust of wind. It was so violent that the map slipped from his fingers and dropped towards the sea below!

If you have it there, remove the MAP from your AIRCRAFT CARD. Now go to 115.

44

As Bertie was reaching into his inside pocket for his map, however, he suddenly noticed some ominous-looking light green patches in the bay that they were fast approaching. Coral! 'Careful, old chap!' he warned Biggles tensely. 'Those rocks look mighty near the surface. They could tear our floats off!' But Biggles just managed to pick out a deep blue channel between the green, and brought the plane safely to a halt. 'That was a close one!' Bertie said with a huge sigh of relief as they rocked gently on the water. *Go to 201.*

45

The Auster now approached Flamingo Island itself. Turning his head a moment to watch the bottle-shaped isle retreat behind them, Ginger suddenly noticed a streak of white cutting through the greenish-blue of one of its bays. He wondered what on earth it was. He would have guessed at a motor-boat – it seemed far too fast for anything else – but how could it be? It was very near where they had just been and they would surely have seen or heard it. But *what* was it, then? He quickly took out his binoculars!

Use your BINOCULARS CARD to obtain a clearer view of this

odd sight by placing it exactly over the shape below – then follow the instruction. If you don't have a BINOCULARS CARD in your AIRCRAFT CARD, go to 79 instead.

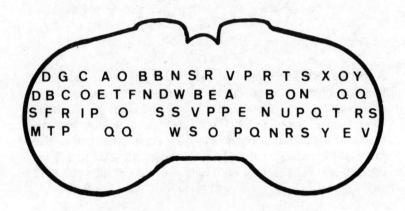

D G C A O B B N S R V P R T S X O Y
D B C O E T F N D W B E A   B O N   Q Q
S F R I P   O   S S V P P E   N U P Q T   R S
M T P   Q Q   W S O   P Q N R S Y E V

46

Just as they were about to start decoding the message on the hut door, however, Biggles thought he heard the sound of an aircraft being revved up. *Theirs!* 'I'm sure it was an Auster engine!' he exclaimed as he immediately led the way back towards their plane. 'Hurry! I think someone might be about to steal it!' But when they finally reached the lagoon it was to see the Auster still innocently waiting there. 'Sorry, it must have been my imagination!' Biggles apologised as they wearily returned to the village. *Go to 225.*

'We need to point ourselves towards the right!' Biggles told the others when he had found north-west with his compass. And, sure enough, twenty minutes later they were back at their plane. They were just about to climb in when Bertie noticed a sheet of paper floating on the shallow water. 'It's another copy of Wolff's codebook!' he remarked with concern as he examined it. 'That suggests that someone else knows about the blueprints – someone who seems to have been snooping round our plane!'

If you don't already have it there, put the CODEBOOK CARD into your AIRCRAFT CARD. Now go to 162.

The Auster had been flying across the island for what must have been a good hour by now but they still hadn't spotted any evidence of Wolff's route. Suddenly, though, as they were passing over a narrow lake, Ginger noticed a small red object near its shore. 'It's a rucksack!' he exclaimed as Biggles brought the plane down towards it so they could have a better look. 'Maybe the trek was getting too hot and arduous for Wolff and he discarded it!' Since the lake appeared to be of a reasonable depth, Biggles thought he had better make a landing . . . *Go to 282.*

'The marsh *is* large enough to be shown!' Ginger declared after finding it on his map. 'It's about ten miles due south of the island's centre.' A quarter of an hour later, the Auster was circling over the marsh, with Biggles trying to decide whether the water was deep enough to enable a landing. 'I'd say yes, old boy,' Bertie recommended. 'Look, even those flamingos at the very edge are standing almost knee-deep!' So Biggles pushed on the control column, starting to take the Auster down . . . *Go to 94.*

The team reached the marsh and their hearts sank when they saw the sheer expanse of it. Their search, if it was to be at all thorough, was likely to take ages! 'If only Wolff's photograph gave some clue as to which part he'd taken it from,' Ginger said with a sigh. 'Something distinctive in the background. But how could it? There *isn't* anything distinctive round here. Just those thousands of flamingos. Not a tree or building in sight!' Or was there? For Biggles thought he could just make out some sort of hut at the far end of the marsh . . . *Go to 156.*

'You don't need your binoculars for that, old boy!' Bertie told Ginger before he had time to unstrap his case. 'I've a much easier way of finding out if that flamingo is real. Watch this!' And with that he suddenly bellowed from the window, scaring all the birds into flight. All except the one that Ginger had been suspicious about, that is. That one remained nonchalantly where it was! The trio immediately decided to go and investigate this phoney bird . . . *Go to 14.*

As Ginger reached into his inside jacket pocket for his map, he noticed that his compass was no longer there. He checked all his other pockets but it wasn't in any of them either. The blessed thing must have dropped out somewhere when he was running along the beach! Still, there was no point dwelling on it . . . and so he returned his attention to the map.

If you have it there, remove the COMPASS CARD from your AIRCRAFT CARD. Now go to 136.

'Spotted it!' Bertie suddenly exclaimed, pointing slightly over to his right. 'See it? You can just make out its humped shape in the haze!' Biggles and Ginger both rubbed their eyes and stared hard at the horizon. They could now see the island too – but only just! It looked as if it might fade away again at any moment! Just in case it did, Biggles asked Ginger to check the direction of the island on his compass. Then it wouldn't matter if it remained visible or not!

Use your COMPASS CARD to find the direction of the island yourself by placing it exactly over the shape below – and with the pointer touching north. Then go to the number that appears in the window. (Remember to return the COMPASS CARD to *your **AIRCRAFT CARD** afterwards.) If you don't have a **COMPASS CARD** in your **AIRCRAFT CARD**, you'll have to guess which of the numbers to go to.*

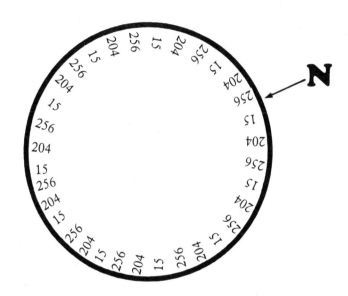

While Ginger and Bertie were both still unstrapping their binoculars cases, however, Biggles gave a despairing chuckle. 'Save yourselves the bother, chaps!' he told them. 'Even if it *is* a rowing-boat down there, the idea of it being Wolff's is just too ridiculous! It would be a heck of a long row from Jamaica. But let's just say he did manage it . . . surely the boat wouldn't be sitting *here*. He would have needed it for his trip back!' As Biggles now started to fly *across* the island, he glanced at the fuel gauge. The pointer was down a quarter already!

Move the pointer on your FUEL GAUGE one coloured segment clockwise. Now go to 158.

55

'The palm-tree's pointing in a north-westerly direction,' Ginger informed the others when he had consulted his compass. 'So I suggest that's the direction we travel across Flamingo Island. There's something not quite natural about the lie of that tree. I'm sure of it!' Biggles was considerably less sure – in fact, the felled tree just looked like a victim of common wind-damage as far as he was concerned – but he quietly followed Ginger's suggestion, banking slightly to the left. North-west was probably just as good a direction as any other, after all! *Go to 205.*

56

Biggles told Ginger he could save him the bother of getting out his map, though. 'See that river-mouth, about four miles to our left?' he asked. 'I remember seeing it on one of the large maps back in Jamaica. It's called the Blue River and it's the only one on the island. Anyway, its mouth is in the south of the island – and so we must be slightly south-east!' *Go to 173.*

'Look, there's some sort of lagoon down to our left,' Biggles said before the village had come much nearer. 'If we were to land there, we wouldn't have too long a trek. But the question is – is the water deep enough for a landing? We don't want to get stuck in half a metre of mud!' While Biggles brought the Auster lower to have a closer look at the lagoon, Ginger suddenly remembered his map. Maybe that would show just how deep it was!

Use your MAP to find which square the lagoon is in – then follow the instruction. If you don't have a MAP in your AIRCRAFT CARD, you'll have to guess which instruction to follow.

If you think D2   go to 217

If you think C2   go to 6

If you think B1   go to 148

Having located the village on his map – it turned out to be the only settlement on the island, so it wasn't very difficult! – Biggles continued to lead the way back towards the bay. They hadn't yet reached the Auster, however, when he stopped again. He had spotted a pair of binoculars on the ground! 'They're in quite good condition–as if they haven't been here that long,' Biggles remarked thoughtfully as he examined them. Anxiety crept into his voice. 'I wonder if that means we're not the only ones hunting for the blueprints!'

If you don't already have it there, put the BINOCULARS CARD into your AIRCRAFT CARD. Now go to 106.

59

While Biggles was opening his copy of Wolff's codebook, Bertie gave the rucksack a gentle scrape to try and remove some of the mud that had dried over the ink-marks. Much to his horror, the canvas just disintegrated in his hand! 'The rucksack has obviously seen too much sun and rain,' Biggles said as they returned, disappointed, to their plane. 'Mind you, at least that proves that it has been there for some while. So it could well have been Wolff's!' Starting the Auster's engine again, Biggles glanced at the instrument panel to check on their fuel situation. The pointer was lower than he'd expected!

Move the pointer on your FUEL GAUGE one coloured segment clockwise. Now go to 71. (Remember: when the pointer reaches the DANGER segment on your FUEL GAUGE, you must immediately stop the game and start all over again from the beginning.)

'What do you think about that small wooden pier down there?' Biggles himself suggested, pointing down to his left. 'Not only is it somewhere to moor the plane but it will also save us getting our feet wet!' As Ginger spotted the pier, however, he didn't feel too confident about it. It looked rather dilapidated, as if it were about to collapse at any moment! He decided to have a closer look at it and so started to unstrap his binoculars case.

Use your BINOCULARS CARD to obtain a clearer view of this pier by placing it exactly over the shape below – then follow the instruction. If you don't have a BINOCULARS CARD in your AIRCRAFT CARD, go to 220 instead.

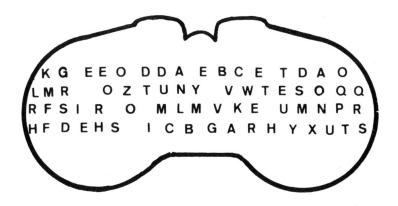

As Bertie started to search his pockets for his copy of Wolff's codebook, however, Biggles suddenly clapped his hand to his forehead! 'Of course!' he exclaimed. 'I knew the name Christen

Hagen rang an odd bell somewhere. It was Werner Wolff's alias!' So the team decided to fly to the waterfall as quickly as possible and bade the woman a hasty goodbye. They were in a bit *too* much of a hurry, though, because Ginger's compass slipped from his pocket as he jumped into the plane!

If you have it there, remove the COMPASS CARD from your AIRCRAFT CARD. Now go to 120.

62

'You need to polish that monocle of yours, Bertie,' Biggles told him with a chuckle before he had had a chance to look through his binoculars. 'Don't you remember, the tree we moored the Auster to bent right over the river. It was the only one that did. Well, there it still is – right next to where you can see our plane!' Bertie rather coyly returned his binoculars to their case and swatted another insect on his arm. 'Blessed things!' he snapped again as they continued towards the marsh. *Go to 50.*

Biggles was the first to reach the part of the beach nearest the shipwreck, the others arriving very soon after him. 'It's a smallish schooner,' he told them as they stared across the few hundred metres of water at its jutting angular bow. 'I should say it's been there a good forty years or so.' They were so engrossed in the wreck that it was quite some time before one of them noticed a large iron box half-embedded in the sand just a few paces away from them . . . *Go to 167.*

'By Jove, the symbols *are* the same!' Bertie exclaimed with delight after he had opened his copy of Wolff's codebook. 'Now, let's work out this message. *GO TO THE ONE THAT IS A FAKE.* What in heaven's name does that mean?' As they were all puzzling over this, Biggles noticed something odd about one of the flamingos outside. It never moved! 'Got it!' he suddenly cried, snapping his fingers. 'That flamingo is the fake the message is referring to. It's just a model!' They were just about to run out and take a good look at this phoney bird when Ginger spotted a compass on the mud floor of the hut. He quickly put it into his pocket . . .

If you don't already have it there, put the COMPASS CARD into your AIRCRAFT CARD. Now go to 14.

Much to the trio's surprise, with a lot of care they *were* able to get behind the waterfall. There was an undercut there, an undercut that was completely dry! 'What a perfect hiding place for Wolff,' Biggles remarked as the water tumbled like a thick screen in front of them. 'Look, we'd be completely unseen from the other side. Now, let's start searching for those blueprints!' A thorough investigation of the undercut didn't reveal any blueprints but it did reveal a small message chiselled into the rock. It read: *WALK FIFTY PACES DUE EAST*.

Use your COMPASS CARD to find this direction by placing it exactly over the shape below – and with the pointer touching north. Then go to the number that appears in the window. If you don't have a COMPASS CARD, you'll have to guess which of the numbers to go to.

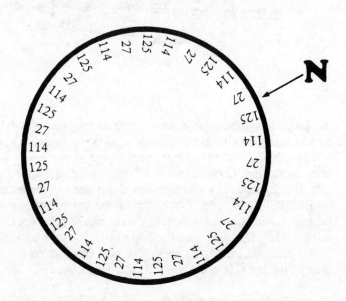

The trio reached the wrecked schooner and clambered aboard. All round them the ship creaked as it was gently rocked by the waves. No wonder the islanders thought it was possessed by evil spirits! They started to explore the part of the ship still above water, treading carefully on the sloping rotten deck. 'Hey, come and look here!' Bertie suddenly called to the others as he examined the stem of the broken foremast. 'Something that could be a coded message has been carved into the wood! Now, where's my copy of Wolff's codebook . . .?'

Use your CODEBOOK CARD to find out what the message means by decoding the instruction below. If you don't have a CODEBOOK CARD in your AIRCRAFT CARD, go to 138 instead.

Bertie changed his mind about getting out his map, though, deciding it could wait a while. His eyes would be better occupied helping Biggles with the landing. If there *were* any light green patches down there and they failed to notice them it could mean ripped floats for the Auster! As Biggles now prepared for the descent towards the water, he happened to notice the fuel gauge. The pointer had dropped a segment already!

Move the pointer on your *FUEL GAUGE* one coloured segment clockwise. Now go to 190.

'We're getting somewhere!' Biggles exclaimed when he had finished decoding the symbols on the scrap of paper. 'It works out as: *WERNER WOLFF CAME TO THIS ISLAND!* What with his cryptic photographs and messages in a bottle, Wolff certainly liked his little games, didn't he?' As Biggles led the way back to their plane so that they could set off again and explore the main part of Flamingo Island, Ginger asked how could he be sure that Wolff wasn't referring to *this* little isle in his message. 'Well, I can't be,' Biggles replied honestly. 'But don't forget that these bottles can drift a long way. Just because it was *found* on this beach it doesn't mean that it was written here!' **Go to 236.**

'It looks as if my hunch was right!' Ginger exclaimed excitedly as the Auster climbed into the air again. 'Did you see that red paint at the side of the smaller cave? It was Wolff's signature beneath some sort of coded message! Fly past again, skip, while I try and jot down the message.' So Biggles put the Auster into a sharp turn, pushing hard on the control column. He flew as slowly as he dared while

Ginger copied the symbols on to the back of his map. As for Bertie – he quickly dug into his inside jacket pocket for his copy of Wolff's codebook!

Use your CODEBOOK CARD to find out what the message says by decoding the instruction below. If you don't have a CODEBOOK CARD in your AIRCRAFT CARD, go to 5 instead.

70

Biggles had second thoughts about using his compass, though. He really couldn't be sure that the old man had any idea what they were talking about. His outstretched arm might simply be pointing them to the nearest water-hole! Biggles was just bidding the old man goodbye when he noticed the yellowed eyes staring wistfully at his binoculars. Deciding to give them to the old man as a gift, Biggles lifted the strap from round his neck!

If you have it there, remove the BINOCULARS CARD from your AIRCRAFT CARD. Now go to 106.

The team continued their aerial search for the blueprints – but the more of the island that passed beneath them, the more hopeless their task seemed. 'Oh, this is impossible!' Bertie finally exclaimed with exasperation. 'I'm beginning to wish that we'd never set eyes on that blessed photograph!' But that remark set Biggles thinking. Of course . . . the *photograph*. Why on earth hadn't he thought of it before! *Go to 187.*

Just as Ginger located the wrecked ship on his map, Biggles joined them in the plane. 'Sorry to keep you,' he said as he leapt into his seat and immediately started up the engine. 'But I noticed the boy waving something at us. It was something he had apparently pick-pocketed from Wolff and kept with him all this time in case it were valuable. He said I could have it for a couple of coins. It seemed an absolute bargain because it was another of Wolff's codebooks!'

If you don't already have it there, put the CODEBOOK CARD into your AIRCRAFT CARD. Now go to 86.

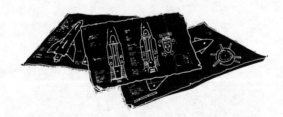

'*THIS IS THE PROPERTY OF WERNER WOLFF!*' Bertie excitedly decoded the symbols on the gun. As he pushed out the cylinder to see if it was loaded – it wasn't – he wondered why Wolff hadn't just had his name engraved in plain English. 'Don't forget, he was a secret service agent,' Biggles reminded him. 'All this cryptography nonsense is a habit with them!' *Go to 50.*

74

'Hang on a second, Bertie!' Ginger objected. 'How do we know that the statue wasn't *meant* to point that way? Perhaps the admiral had a house or was buried in that direction across the island? There could be all sorts of reasons for it!' But Bertie insisted it was decidedly odd. Statues of admirals always looked out to sea! ***Go to 213.***

75

'Wait a second,' Ginger objected. 'How do we know that the flamingos aren't flying away from the marsh rather than towards it?' Bertie replied that they didn't – that was all part of the fun! 'Now, hurry up and take out that compass,' he added with a chuckle. ***Go to 144.***

76

'Has my compass dropped out somewhere?' Ginger asked himself with a frown when he couldn't find it in his inside jacket pocket. He took out the map that was there so he could have a better search. Suddenly, though, a fierce gust of wind tore through the dilapidated hut, carrying the map out through the open doorway. The map was deposited right out of reach in the marshy water! The news about Ginger's compass was rather better, though, for he suddenly found it in another of his pockets.

If you have it there, remove the MAP from your AIRCRAFT CARD. Now go to 111.

'How about that small bay down there?' Ginger suggested when they had followed the island's coastline for a mile or two. 'The one with all those high sand-dunes. The sea looks very calm there and it's also quite a strong blue, so it should be deep enough for landing!' While Biggles checked that Ginger was right – making absolutely sure there weren't any light green patches which might mean rocks – Bertie decided to look for the sand-dunes on his map. It would tell them exactly where they were.

Use your MAP to find which square the bay with the sand-dunes is in – then follow the instruction. If you don't have a MAP in your AIRCRAFT CARD, you'll have to guess which instruction to follow.

If you think E1	go to 67
If you think E3	go to 190
If you think E2	go to 30

'Well, well, well!' Bertie exclaimed when he had consulted his codebook. 'These symbols *are* a message! It says that the blueprints are hidden somewhere on Flamingo Island!' He would have liked it to have been rather more precise but at least it confirmed that they had come to the right place! Biggles had decided to cut the Auster's engine and glide the rest of the crossing to Flamingo Island, firstly to save a bit of fuel, and secondly because Ginger thought he could hear another aircraft in the sky. He searched all round for it, worried that they were being followed; but there was nothing to be seen. Either his ears had been deceiving him – or the aircraft was very clever at keeping itself hidden! *Go to 228.*

79

By the time Ginger had focused his binoculars, however, the streak of white had disappeared! 'Maybe it was just a freak wave, old boy,' Bertie said to him . . . but Ginger was now almost certain that it *had* been a motor-boat. A motor-boat they hadn't seen because *it didn't want to be seen*! A motor-boat that was perhaps following them! Ginger kept his troubled thoughts to himself, though, turning his eyes to the front once more. 'We're a quarter down on our juice already,' Biggles remarked as he glanced at the plane's fuel gauge. 'Let's hope we don't have to do too much zig-zagging across this island or it'll never last out!'

Move the pointer on your FUEL GAUGE one coloured segment clockwise. Now go to 228.

80

Biggles led the way towards the base of the mountain and also along the narrow track that climbed to its top. 'Ginger, it looks as if you've hit the bull's-eye!' he exclaimed some two hours later when they finally reached the wooden cross. 'Someone's carved what could be a coded message into the wood. Who's putting their money on our friend Wolff?' Well, Biggles himself certainly was . . . and so he immediately reached into his pocket for his copy of Wolff's codebook.

Use your CODEBOOK CARD to find out what the message says by decoding the instruction below. If you don't have a CODEBOOK CARD in your AIRCRAFT CARD, go to 19 instead.

But before Bertie had had a chance to focus his binoculars on the helicopter it had drifted off, flying away from the island. 'Well, let's just hope that that proves it was perfectly innocent,' Biggles remarked. He was still a little uneasy about it, though. Perhaps it had just disappeared temporarily – so they didn't become suspicious! Biggles was also growing uneasy about the fuel situation. Glancing at the gauge, he noticed that the pointer had dropped once more.

Move the pointer on your FUEL GAUGE one coloured segment clockwise. Now go to 71. (Remember: when the pointer reaches the DANGER segment on your FUEL GAUGE, you must immediately stop the game and start all over again from the beginning.)

Biggles turned the Auster round above this jagged corner of the coastline, heading back towards the mountain. It seemed more sense to explore the area on its other side. There was obviously considerably more of the island there. Whether they would have enough fuel for much of this exploring, though, was an entirely different matter. For, glancing down at the gauge, Biggles saw that the pointer was rather lower than he'd hoped!

Move the pointer on your FUEL GAUGE one coloured segment clockwise. Now go to 71. (Remember: when the pointer reaches the DANGER segment on your FUEL GAUGE, you must immediately stop the game and start all over again from the beginning.)

Ginger reached the Auster first, Bertie just behind him. Biggles had suddenly stopped about halfway, though, and turned back towards the boy. He'd realised that they had forgotten to ask him a very important question: in which direction was this wrecked ship? The boy answered by pointing a thin, shiny arm towards the horizon. Biggles immediately reached into his pocket so he could check this direction on his compass.

Use your COMPASS CARD to work out the direction the boy is indicating by placing it exactly over the shape below – and with the pointer touching north. Then go to the number that appears in the window. If you don't have a COMPASS CARD, you'll have to guess which of the numbers to go to.

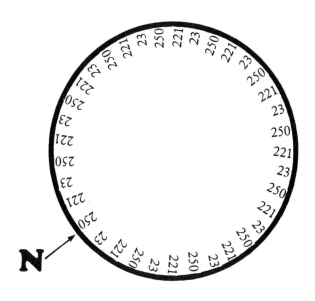

84

Ginger studied his map but he couldn't find any rocks in this part of
the river. So either there weren't any . . . or the person who had
drawn the map hadn't bothered to show them! Well, they would
soon find out which because Biggles was now touching down on the
river, the Auster's floats skidding across the surface. Ginger
prepared himself for a bump but the plane came smoothly to a stop,
just metres from the right bank. *Go to 109.*

85

'There's the waterfall!' the woman said as she pointed to it on
Ginger's map. Her teeth gleamed as she grinned proudly at them.
'That's where the man hid!' Much to the trio's surprise, she then
delved into the folds of her dress for a little notebook. 'I saw him
drop this,' she told Ginger with a friendly smile. 'You can take it!'
Having thanked the woman for her help, the team quickly climbed
back into their plane so they could fly to the waterfall. It was only
once they were in the air that Ginger saw what was in the little
notebook. Another list of Wolff's codes!

*If you don't already have it there, put the CODEBOOK CARD
into your AIRCRAFT CARD. Now go to 197.*

A short while later the team were following the coastline again, keeping their eyes skinned for this wrecked ship. 'I wonder how much of the ship is above water?' Biggles asked as he flew at the minimum speed possible. 'Enough for us to be able to spot her, I hope!' Bertie started to unstrap his binoculars case, thinking they might help in the search . . .

Use your BINOCULARS CARD to try and locate the ship-wreck by placing it exactly over the shape below – then follow the instruction. If you don't have a BINOCULARS CARD in your AIRCRAFT CARD, go to 96 instead.

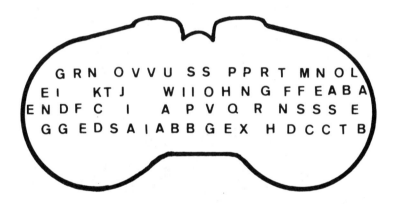

Biggles didn't quite share his team-mates' conviction about the arrow, though. He thought it might just be a blemish in the rock. So Ginger left his compass where it was for a moment while Biggles made another swoop past the caves. 'I see what you mean, skip,' Ginger admitted. 'It really doesn't look like an arrow at all now! It's obviously just a small fault in the cliff-face that's become discoloured.' **Go to 206.**

88

Before Ginger had time to check the direction of the village on his compass, however, the Auster was already down, skating to a halt just short of the beach. As it turned out, the few huts *were* still visible now that they had landed and so the compass reading wasn't necessary. 'We should reach them in about twenty minutes,' Biggles said as they paddled through the warm water to the shore. *Go to 33.*

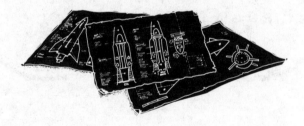

89

The river became narrower and narrower, faster and faster, until the waterfall suddenly appeared ahead. 'Gosh, look at the size of it!' Ginger exclaimed as he stared up at its three cascading tiers, the lowest one a good thirty metres across. 'Go any nearer and we'll be soaked!' But go nearer they must – because the woman at the marsh had told them that Wolff had actually gone *behind* the waterfall. It didn't really seem possible – not without risk of drowning, anyway – but they slowly made their way forward across the slippery rocks . . . *Go to 65.*

Only a few minutes after the Auster had alighted on the river, the trio were wading towards its bank. 'You might have stopped a bit closer to it, old chap,' Bertie joked. 'This is going to ruin my socks!' His humour soon went, however, when Ginger asked apprehensively if any water-snakes were known to inhabit this island. 'Gosh, I hope not!' Bertie exclaimed as they all raced for dry ground.

Throw the SPECIAL DICE to determine who is to reach it first.

BIGGLES thrown	go to 200
BERTIE thrown	go to 254
GINGER thrown	go to 223

91

'But there could be *hundreds* of banana plantations on this island, old boy!' Bertie told Ginger before he had a chance to open his map. 'How will you know that you've got the right one?' This was something that in his enthusiasm Ginger hadn't considered – and so he disappointedly returned his map to his inside pocket. As he did so, he noticed that his compass was no longer there. It wasn't in any of his other pockets or by his feet either. 'Blow!' he exclaimed. 'It must have dropped out somewhere back in Jamaica!'

If you have it there, remove the COMPASS CARD from your AIRCRAFT CARD. Now go to 173.

92

The very last thing the trio were expecting to find on the beach was a message in a bottle . . . but that is exactly what they did find! 'Desert islands and a message in a bottle!' Bertie remarked with disbelief as Biggles picked it up. 'It seems so absurdly corny!' Biggles pulled the folded sheet of paper out, pressing it flat. 'The message seems to be in some sort of code!' he said as he reached into his inside jacket pocket. 'Now, where's my copy of Wolff's codebook?'

Use your CODEBOOK CARD to find out what the message says by decoding the instruction below. If you don't have a CODEBOOK CARD in your AIRCRAFT CARD, go to 169 instead.

When the plane was level with the piece of wood, however, Bertie saw that the strange symbols painted on it weren't symbols at all! 'It says: *BEWARE OF DEEP WATER*,' he told them in embarrassment as he leaned out of his window to read it. 'It's obviously just an old sign and the paint's peeling off!' Biggles was now ready to switch off the plane's engine so they could wade the few metres to the lagoon's edge. But before he did, he checked the fuel gauge. The pointer was rather lower than he'd hoped!

Move the pointer on your FUEL GAUGE one coloured segment clockwise. Now go to 224.

The flamingos all rose screaming into the air as the Auster ploughed through them across the marshy water, skidding to a halt. The team had hardly stepped down from the plane when a large woman with gleaming white teeth appeared. She was furious! 'Stop scaring my birds!' she ranted. 'Those flamingos are my responsibility. They won't breed if they're scared. You're just like the other man who landed here some while back!' The trio suddenly became very attentive. Could she be referring to Wolff? *Go to 26.*

95

Biggles told Bertie that they couldn't afford the time to decode the symbols on the gun, however. 'There aren't many hours of daylight left,' he said, glancing at his watch. 'And we're probably going to need every minute we have to explore the marsh. Take the gun with you and we can have another look at it later.' They hadn't walked much further when Bertie suddenly tripped over a rock. He held his breath as he fell, praying that the gun wasn't loaded – it could well go off in his pocket! Fortunately, it didn't, but his binoculars shattered as he hit the hard ground.

If you have it there, remove the BINOCULARS CARD from your AIRCRAFT CARD. Now go to 50.

96

'That's her!' Biggles suddenly cried before Bertie even had time to take out his binoculars. 'See? About half a mile ahead, some four hundred metres from the shore. It's not a very large ship but I reckon a good half of it must be above the water.' As they neared the shipwreck, Biggles glanced at the instrument panel to check on their fuel situation. The pointer had dropped quite a bit since he last looked!

Move the pointer on your FUEL GAUGE one coloured segment clockwise. Now go to 186. (Remember: when the pointer reaches the DANGER segment on your FUEL GAUGE, you must immediately stop the game and start all over again from the beginning.)

'They've seen us coming!' Biggles panted as the men suddenly broke away from the Auster and ran for the cover of the palms. 'Let's just hope they didn't have time to do any damage.' Fortunately, they didn't – but Biggles was still deeply troubled by what had taken place. 'Those men are obviously interested in the blueprints as well, and are trying to thwart our search,' he said as he finished his quick check of the plane. 'Well, for the time being, I think we're going to have to let them have their way. They're almost certainly armed for one thing. The wisest course of action would be to return to Jamaica and get ourselves better protected. We'll just have to hope that in the meantime they don't discover the blueprints first!'

Your mission wasn't successful, unfortunately. If you would like another attempt at it, you must start the game all over again from the beginning. Try setting off with a different EQUIPMENT CARD this time to see if it gives you any more luck!

Only seconds before the Auster came in sight through the trees, however, the noise stopped. 'Whoever it was must have given up with her and fled,' Biggles remarked when they had hurried right up to their aircraft and found no one there. 'They presumably didn't know enough about planes.' But he was soon to find that the person must have known at least a *little* about them. For when he restarted the Auster's engine, he saw that the fuel level was considerably lower than it had been before. Some of the fuel had obviously been siphoned off!

Move the pointer on your FUEL GAUGE one coloured segment clockwise. Now go to 162.

99

'It says that the blueprints are hidden in the direction that the knife is pointing!' Bertie exclaimed when he had decoded the scratched message. 'That's straight ahead, the way we're going. So it looks, old chaps, as if the waterfall *is* the hiding-place!' Biggles' delight wasn't quite as complete as his friend's, though, for he thought of something that Bertie hadn't considered. During the long time that it had been lying there, the knife might well have been accidentally twisted round! *Go to 89.*

Biggles remained in the plane while Bertie and Ginger clambered out on to the pier. 'You know, if Wolff came to the island by boat,' Ginger remarked eagerly as they carefully walked along the rotting wooden structure, 'this might well have been where he landed. Let's keep our eyes skinned in case he dropped something – a watch or cigarette case perhaps!' Bertie was most doubtful about this possibility but then he suddenly stopped on one of the planks. A number of symbols had been carved into it – could it be a coded message? He immediately dug into his jacket pocket for his copy of Wolff's codebook . . .

*Use your **CODEBOOK CARD** to find out what the symbols mean by decoding the instruction below. If you don't have a **CODEBOOK CARD** in your **AIRCRAFT CARD**, go to 233 instead.*

'It works out as: *MAP HIDDEN INSIDE,*' Bertie eagerly informed the others when he had used his codebook to make sense of the symbols on the buoy. He immediately climbed out of his door and wedged himself in the wing supports so that he could reach down for the buoy. 'It must be made up of two parts,' he said as he started to twist the top half of the plastic sphere. 'Yes, here it comes! A blessed shame it's not the blueprints themselves hidden inside. Although doubtless the map will show where they are!' Sadly, though, it didn't. For as hard as he studied the map Bertie couldn't find a single cross or arrow marked on it! 'Well, at least the hiding of the map suggests that Wolff definitely *did* come to this area,' said Biggles, trying to console them all as the Auster lifted into the air again. 'I can't think why anyone else would have gone to such trouble as that!'

If you don't already have it there, put the MAP into your AIRCRAFT CARD. Now go to 45.

'No, forget your binoculars!' Biggles said, suddenly changing his mind before Ginger had time to remove them from their case. 'It could take you ages to search every inch of sky. I've got a much better idea!' He quietened the engine for a moment so they could all *listen* for the plane. 'Yes, there it is!' Biggles exclaimed, cupping his hand behind his ear. 'Quite a small bird by the sound of it, like ours. Now I wonder what it's up to? I think I'll go on a bit of a jaunt to see if it follows us!' *Go to 13.*

Biggles now started to fly *across* the island, the statue getting smaller behind them. But, before the stone admiral completely disappeared, Ginger thought it might be a good idea to look for it on his map. It would show them exactly which part of the island they were in.

Use your MAP to find which square the statue is in – then follow the instruction. If you don't have a MAP in your AIRCRAFT CARD, you'll have to guess which instruction to follow.

If you think C4	go to 56
If you think D4	go to 18
If you think D3	go to 173

Ginger's compass showed that the village was slightly south-east of where they were about to alight. It was fortunate he had taken this reading because, when the Auster reached the level of the bay, all they could see on the shore was a dense screen of palm-trees – the village was completely obscured! 'Slightly south-east you say, Ginger?' Biggles checked, as following his compass he led the way through the trees. *Go to 33.*

'I doubt whether Wolff would have used the left cave for his hiding-place, old chap,' Bertie told Biggles after he'd peered into it through his binoculars. 'There are far too many sharp rocks sticking out of the water. They would rip a boat to shreds!' Since Ginger said the same was true of the right cave, Biggles decided the caves could now be safely ruled out of their search. He therefore took the plane up into the air again, turning it to fly across the island. *Go to 48.*

A short while later the village became just a few dots again as the Auster lifted the team back into the sky. They hadn't flown very far, however, when Ginger spotted that they weren't alone up there. Several miles to their left flitted a helicopter! 'I wonder what it's up to?' Biggles asked suspiciously. 'I hope it's not tailing us! Bertie, take a look at it through your binoculars, will you, and see what type of chopper it is.'

Use your BINOCULARS CARD to obtain a clearer vie:v of the helicopter by placing it exactly over the shape below – then follow the instruction. If you don't have a BINOCULARS CARD in your AIRCRAFT CARD, go to 81 instead.

```
U G Y V O T T U P N R S Q T N N O M
S T R   W Y O V V U   V N S P P E M M
 T S N Z H R U T I S N R R E T S S E P
R FT  T I S T R V   Y U W P E Y O U
```

'The flamingos are flying virtually due south,' Ginger told his skipper when he had consulted his compass. So Biggles banked the plane until due south was showing on *its* compass. They didn't have to fly in this direction for long before they suddenly spotted the marsh ahead of them, the flamingos now dropping down towards it. **Go to 22.**

Biggles' compass showed that the woman was pointing in a north-westerly direction to the waterfall. He was just about to thank her for her help when she suddenly waddled off towards a small reed hut further round the marsh. But a few minutes later she was back with them. 'While I was following that man to the waterfall,' she told Biggles proudly, handing him a little notebook, 'I noticed he dropped this. I picked it up and kept it!' Quickly flicking through the notebook, Biggles saw that it was another copy of Wolff's codes!

If you don't already have it there, put the CODEBOOK CARD into your AIRCRAFT CARD. Now go to 210.

A few minutes later the trio were mooring the Auster to a palm-tree growing on the river-bank. They then immediately set off towards the marsh. 'These blessed insects,' Bertie complained as they went. 'I'm being bitten all over!' On turning his head to deal with a particularly nasty specimen that had landed on the back of his arm, Bertie glimpsed their plane which was now a small speck some half-mile behind them. He was sure it had moved along the river! 'Don't tell me it's broken away from its moorings!' he cried, quickly reaching for his binoculars so he could check.

Use your BINOCULARS CARD to obtain a clearer view of the Auster by placing it exactly over the shape below – then follow the instruction. If you don't have a BINOCULARS CARD in your AIRCRAFT CARD, go to 62 instead.

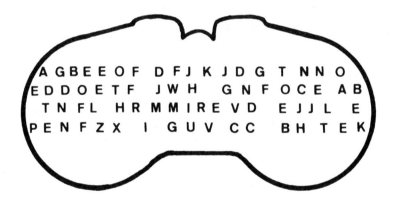

Having found the waterfall on his map, Ginger looked for any contour lines nearby so that he could work out roughly what sort of drop it had. 'Here's one,' he said thoughtfully. 'Three hundred metres above sea-level. And here's another, right at the bottom of the waterfall – one hundred metres. That must mean the drop's about two hundred metres. In other words, the waterfall's quite a large one!' ***Go to 153.***

111

Ginger was just removing his compass from his pocket when there was a terrific noise outside the hut. The flamingos had all suddenly taken to the air! 'Perhaps we're not the only people on the marsh!' Bertie said anxiously as they all rushed outside to investigate. They certainly couldn't *see* anyone else there – but as they were returning to the hut, Biggles noticed something rather odd. One of the flamingos had stayed behind, firmly rooted to the spot! 'I'm not so sure that really is a flamingo!' he exclaimed as he led the way towards it to take a closer look. ***Go to 14.***

112

Less than twenty minutes later, the trio were back at their plane, immediately climbing in so that they could set off to explore other parts of the island. 'My mountain suggestion wasn't such a good one after all, was it?' Ginger said apologetically as they now rose up into the air again. 'Wolff was obviously a lot craftier than I gave him credit for!' ***Go to 162.***

113

Ginger had only just started unfolding his map, however, when Biggles returned. 'We forgot to ask the boy where the wrecked ship was!' he said, explaining his delay, as he took his seat. 'I also thought he deserved a small payment for his help. He promised in return that there would be no more stealing of the flamingo eggs. I'm not sure I believe him but we can always hope!' ***Go to 86.***

'Do you think this message was chiselled by Wolff?' Ginger asked excitedly as they read it again. 'And, if it was, do you think the *blueprints* are at the end of these fifty paces?' The others really weren't sure. But there was only one way that they could be . . . that was to start counting the fifty paces! *Go to 27.*

'Now the really hard part begins!' Bertie commented cynically as the hump of land came nearer and nearer, growing more colourful. 'Finding the island might have been a piece of cake but finding the blueprints certainly won't be! Where on earth do we start?' Reducing the plane's height, Biggles could only suggest that they look out for some evidence of Wolff's landing there. A discarded life-jacket on a beach, for instance – or a torn sail. It would be a chance in a million, of course, but they could always hope!

Throw the SPECIAL DICE to determine who is to spot something that might be evidence.

BIGGLES thrown	go to 139
BERTIE thrown	go to 17
GINGER thrown	go to 234

116

Bertie was still searching for his codebook when a sudden gust of wind passed through the Auster's cockpit. It lifted the photograph of the flamingo right off Bertie's lap, spinning it out through the open window! 'Blow!' he exclaimed as he helplessly watched it drift down towards the sea below. *Go to 283.*

117

'Look, the village isn't that far from the sea,' Ginger said, pointing a mile or so to the right of the huts. 'We could put down in that sheltered bay over there. It would only mean a short hike!' As Biggles turned the Auster towards the bay, depressing the right rudder pedal, Ginger took out his compass, thinking he had better check the direction of the village from the bay. This was just in case the few huts were no longer visible when they landed!

Use your COMPASS CARD to find the direction of the village

*from the sea yourself by placing it exactly over the shape below –
and with the pointer touching north. Then go to the number that
appears in the window. If you don't have a COMPASS CARD,
you'll have to guess which of the numbers to go to.*

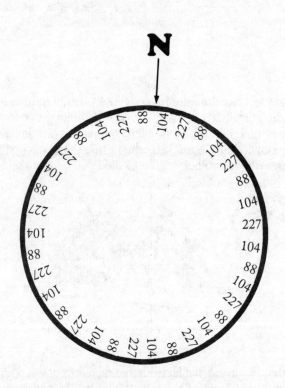

118

'I'm sorry to disappoint you, Bertie,' Biggles told him before he
could take out his binoculars, 'but I'm afraid your hunch about
Wolff arriving by parachute has a flaw! To have parachuted on to

the island, he would have needed an accomplice to fly the plane. But it's highly unlikely that Wolff would have trusted an accomplice. Not with the blueprints being so valuable!' As Biggles continued his journey inland, searching for a more likely clue, he shared some of Bertie's despondency. Apart from anything else, the pointer on the fuel gauge seemed to drop every time he glanced at it!

Move the pointer on your FUEL GAUGE one coloured segment clockwise. Now go to 48.

Move the pointer on your FUEL GAUGE one coloured segment clockwise. Now go to 48.

119

The roll of negatives suddenly flapped out of Ginger's fingers, though, caught by a gust of wind. It wasn't blown far but far enough to reach the water's edge. 'Drat, the negatives are ruined!' Ginger exclaimed as he quickly paddled into the lake after them. 'And so's that coded message on them!' There was more bad news in store for the team. As their plane climbed into the air again, Biggles noticed that the fuel gauge was reading much lower than it should have done. That snooper had obviously siphoned off some fuel!

Move the pointer on your FUEL GAUGE one coloured segment clockwise. Now go to 162.

Move the pointer on your FUEL GAUGE one coloured segment clockwise. Now go to 162.

'I've just realised something!' Biggles exclaimed with despair as they now left the marsh behind. 'We forgot to ask the woman where the waterfall *was*!' They all scanned the scenery ahead of them in the hope that they might spot it but all they could see was a large derelict house. 'Look it up on your map, will you, Ginger,' Biggles asked. 'We'll at least know exactly where we are then!'

Use your MAP to find which square the large house is in – then follow the instruction. If you don't have a MAP in your AIRCRAFT CARD, you'll have to guess which instruction to follow.

If you think A3	go to 40
If you think A2	go to 272
If you think B3	go to 239

'You can stop circling round now, thanks, skip,' Ginger told Biggles disappointedly as he studied the purplish patch of water through his binoculars. 'I think it's just a bit of the reef down there that's making the sea darker. I'm convinced it's not a ship, anyway!' Ginger was even more sure a few seconds later when he raised his head, happening to look half a mile or so further along the coast. Sticking out of the water was the whole of a ship's bow. *That* was the shipwreck! **Go to 186.**

122

'It's a plastic model!' Ginger exclaimed as he focused his binoculars on the flamingo. 'A pretty realistic one – but definitely a model. Its plumage is too shiny!' They were just about to rush out and investigate this bizarre model more closely when Biggles spotted a compass on the floor of the hut. Perhaps Wolff *had* sheltered there after all!

If you don't already have it there, put the COMPASS CARD into your AIRCRAFT CARD. Now go to 14.

123

This part of the bay was indeed a good spot to put down because the Auster alighted without problem. The trio sat there for a few moments, waiting for the gently-lapping waves to float the plane into the shallows. They then leapt out on to the beach and hurried along the white sand towards the part that was directly opposite the shipwreck.

Throw the SPECIAL DICE to decide who is to reach it first.

BIGGLES thrown	go to 63
BERTIE thrown	go to 177
GINGER thrown	go to 241

Biggles was just taking his compass from his pocket, however, when the old man lifted his arm to the sky. He seemed to be pointing at some small clouds that had appeared. Maybe he was trying to tell them that a storm was gathering – but whatever it was, it clearly had nothing to do with Wolff! So after waving the old man goodbye, the team started on their journey back to the plane. If it *was* a storm the old man was trying to tell them about, they had better get moving! ***Go to 106.***

Using one of their compasses to find due east from the rock, the trio eagerly started counting the fifty paces. It took them to the side of the waterfall and then out to just beyond the catchment pool. There, lying on the dampish ground, was another rock! They all stared down at it, none of them daring to turn it over. Could the blueprints really be underneath? 'Oh, this is ridiculous!' Biggles remarked, and he immediately lifted up the rock. Bertie and Ginger both held their breath as he brought out a slim, metallic tube that had been pressed into the soil beneath it. 'Well done, team!' Biggles exclaimed delightedly after he had unscrewed the top of the tube and extracted several tight rolls of paper. 'Look – the blueprints!'

And well done to YOU too. You have successfully completed the mission!

As Bertie was reaching into his inside jacket pocket for his copy of Wolff's codebook, however, a fierce gust of wind suddenly passed through the dilapidated hut. It whipped the film packet off the floor, carrying it out over the marsh! The trio ran out after it, causing the flamingos to take to the air in a noisy bright pink cloud. All except one, that was. This remained nonchalantly rooted to the spot! 'You know, I don't think that one's real!' Biggles remarked, deciding to go and examine it . . . ***Go to 14.***

'There's the island!' Ginger suddenly exclaimed, pointing directly ahead of him, between Biggles and Bertie. 'I can just make out a greyish hump on the horizon!' But as hard as Biggles and Bertie stared in the direction Ginger's finger was pointing, they could see nothing but haze. 'Either we need our eyes testing,' Bertie told Ginger with a chuckle, 'or you're just imagining things, old boy! Anyway, I'll soon tell you which. I'll take a look through my binoculars!'

Use your BINOCULARS CARD to obtain a clearer view of the

horizon by placing it exactly over the shape below – then follow the instruction. If you don't have a *BINOCULARS CARD* in your *AIRCRAFT CARD*, go to 43 instead.

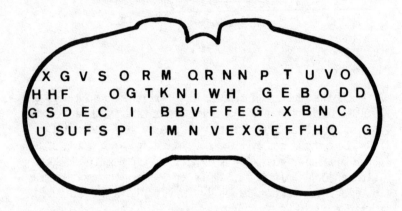

128

As Ginger was taking out his compass, however, Biggles noticed several more fallen palms a little further along the beach. And they were all pointing in that same direction! 'I'm afraid that puts an end to your arrow theory, Ginger!' he told him. 'It was obviously the work of the wind after all. Unless of course you're suggesting that Wolff went along felling every one of the trees!' As Biggles now put the bottle-shaped isle behind them, heading across the straits for Flamingo Island itself, he glanced down at the fuel gauge. They had emptied a quarter of their tank already!

Move the pointer on your FUEL GAUGE one coloured segment clockwise. Now go to 205.

129

'The harbour's on the north-east corner of the island,' Ginger informed the others when he had located it on his map. Returning the map to his jacket pocket, he wondered when the harbour had last been in use. 'Judging by those rotten piers,' Bertie answered, 'certainly not in the last fifty years! In fact, I'd say the harbour hasn't seen much activity since the previous century. There must have been some export business going on then. Sugar, perhaps, or bananas.' *Go to 236.*

130

Bertie led the way towards the mountain, the others only a step or so behind him. It took a good two hours for them to reach the top – two hours that were wasted because there was absolutely no sign of the blueprints up there! They were despondently making their way down again when Biggles suddenly halted. He pointed below at the small shape that was their plane. 'Isn't that someone snooping round it?' he asked anxiously, squinting hard. 'Let me get out my binoculars!'

Use your BINOCULARS CARD to obtain a clearer view of the

plane by placing it exactly over the shape below – then follow the instruction. If you don't have a *BINOCULARS CARD* in your *AIRCRAFT CARD*, go to 258 instead.

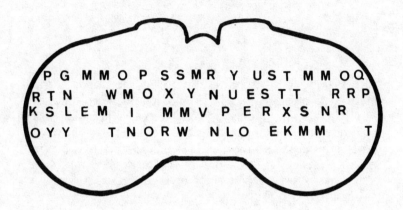

131

'*BLUEPRINTS HIDDEN NO MORE THAN TWENTY MILES AWAY!*' Bertie told the others ecstatically when he had used his codebook to work out what the symbols on the hut door said. 'It's just the sort of clue we've been hoping for!' But his excitement subsided a little when Biggles pointed out that a twenty mile radius encompassed a good half of the island. 'It's certainly better than nothing,' Biggles added as they now returned to their plane at the lagoon. 'But it would have been a lot nicer if the message had specified *which direction* the miles were in!' **Go to 106.**

132

'Well, it's not an official one, that's for sure!' Bertie said as he focused his binoculars on the helicopter. 'If it were fire-brigade or army, it would be a lot bigger. This chopper's quite a tiddler, though – the sort that's privately owned.' Removing his monocle, he gave it a quick clean. 'Oh, not to worry, old chaps!' he reassured them as he took another look through his binoculars. 'The chopper's gone.' Biggles only hoped that it was for good! ***Go to 71.***

133

'I'll wager that *that's* where the marsh is!' Bertie exclaimed, suddenly pointing to his right. 'Look, there's a flock of flamingos flying that way. Can you see them? Those pink specks about two miles away!' Biggles decided to turn the plane towards the flamingos but just in case he lost sight of them during the manoeuvre he asked Ginger to check the direction they were flying on his compass.

Use your COMPASS CARD to find which way the flamingos are flying by placing it exactly over the shape below – and with the

*pointer touching north. **Then go to the number that appears in the window. If you don't have a COMPASS CARD, you'll have to guess which of the numbers to go to.***

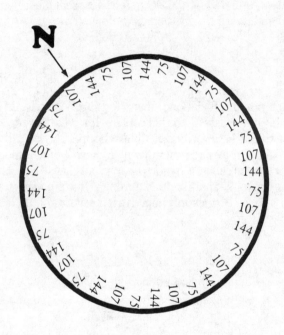

'Did this man give his name?' Ginger asked, just before the others. The woman started by shaking her head, but then she glanced at the expensive-looking watch on her wrist. She took it off. 'His name was Christen Hagen!' she answered, delightedly showing them the engraving on the back of the watch. 'Do you see? He gave this to me and made me promise not to tell anyone that he'd been here. That's how I knew he was up to no good!' The team were, of course, rather disappointed to see that the name wasn't Wolff's . . . but then Bertie noticed that there was some more engraving just beneath it. Engraving that was not letters but the symbols of a code!

Use your CODEBOOK CARD to find out what these symbols mean by decoding the instruction below. If you don't have a CODEBOOK CARD in your AIRCRAFT CARD, go to 61 instead.

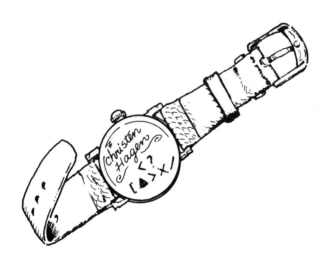

Focusing his binoculars on the Auster, however, Bertie was relieved to see that it was still firmly moored to the tree. 'It must be this blessed monocle of mine!' he said with annoyance, removing it from his eye to give it a thorough wipe. 'Perhaps it's time I invested in a new one!' The trio hadn't walked much further towards the marsh when Ginger noticed a sun-bleached notebook on the ground. He picked it up, carefully opening the frail pages. 'Wolff must also have passed this way,' he exclaimed to the others. 'Look, it's full of those codes of his! He obviously had more than just the one copy.'

If you don't already have it there, put the CODEBOOK CARD into your AIRCRAFT CARD. Now go to 50.

136
Before Ginger could open his map, however, Biggles and Bertie arrived. 'Looks as if she was once quite a little beauty, doesn't she?' Bertie remarked as he stared across at the shipwreck, polishing his monocle in appreciation. 'A fore-and-aft schooner, if I'm not mistaken! Probably fifty or sixty years old. I know that sort of sailing-ship was quite common in this part of the world then.' *Go to 264.*

137
Bertie pointed out that they didn't need a map, though. All they had to do to find out which part of the coast they were at, was to look at the plane's compass. 'It's showing north-west,' he said, reading it for them. 'So this must be the north-west corner of the island!' *Go to 82.*

138
Just as Bertie was taking out his copy of Wolff's codebook, however, Ginger gave a cry of alarm. 'Look!' he shouted, pointing along the beach to where their plane was moored. 'The Auster! There are some men walking up to it with what appear to be flaming branches in their hands. I do believe they mean to set fire to it!' The team immediately jumped into their little boat, rowing for all they were worth back to the shore. Then they dashed the half-mile or so towards the plane . . . *Go to 97.*

'Is that an upturned boat on the sand?' Biggles asked suddenly as they now flew over the island's shore. He banked sharply to the left, circling round. 'Do you see it – a greyish hump, like the keel of a rowing-boat? Perhaps that was how Wolff travelled to the island. And if it was, maybe he left some sort of clue inside!' He asked the others to have a quick look through their binoculars to make absolutely sure it was a rowing-boat.

Use your BINOCULARS CARD to obtain a clearer view of the greyish hump by placing it exactly over the shape below – then follow the instruction. If you don't have a BINOCULARS CARD in your AIRCRAFT CARD, go to 54 instead.

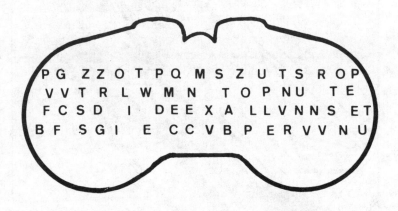

140

'We're at the north-east corner of Flamingo Island,' Bertie announced when he had located the key-shaped isle on his map. But all of Biggles' attention was on the water that they were fast approaching. He hadn't noticed it when they were higher up, but there was a huge purple area directly beneath them. Was it surface coral? If it was, then their whole undercarriage could be wrecked! He was just about to jerk back the control column to try and avoid the landing when the purple patch dispersed in front of him. It was just a shoal of fish! *Go to 201.*

141

'It *is* a motor-boat, after all!' Ginger remarked bewilderedly as he focused his binoculars. 'Well, why on earth didn't we notice it when we were down there? Perhaps it's deliberately keeping out of sight, secretly following us!' But Bertie told him not to let his imagination run away with him. 'I dare say it's just a tourist on a day's outing from Jamaica,' he remarked simply. 'How *can* anyone be following us? We couldn't have kept this mission more hush-hush!' *Go to 228.*

142

'Well, there's certainly no one here now, old chap,' Bertie panted as they finally reached the Auster. 'He seems to have scarpered!' They were having a quick kneel-down at the lake's edge to recover their breath when Ginger spotted a roll of film negatives in the grass. Holding it up to the sun, he saw that one of the negatives was exactly the same shot as the photograph that they had – the flamingo standing in a marsh! What was more, there were some symbols inked across the frame. Sure that it was some sort of code, Ginger quickly reached into his pocket for his copy of Wolff's codebook!

*Use your **CODEBOOK CARD** to find out what the symbols mean by decoding the instruction below. If you don't have a **CODEBOOK CARD** in your **AIRCRAFT CARD**, go to 119 instead.*

143

'I was right!' Bertie declared when he had quickly cast a monocled eye over his copy of Wolff's codebook. 'It *is* a coded message on that piece of wood! It works out as: *HEAD WEST FOR BLUE-PRINTS!*' Unfortunately, a good two thirds of the island was *west* of the lagoon but it narrowed their search a little! ***Go to 224.***

By the time Ginger had produced his compass, however, Biggles had completed his turn towards the flock of flamingos. They were now directly in front of him! 'Seems as if you've won that wager, Bertie,' Biggles told him after a few minutes of following the exotic birds. 'There's the marsh just ahead of them. Look, they're starting to land!' As the Auster approached the marsh, Biggles checked his fuel gauge. The pointer was rather lower than he would have liked!

Move the pointer on your FUEL GAUGE one coloured segment clockwise. Now go to 22.

The team hadn't flown much further along the coast when Ginger noticed a dark patch in the sea below. The sea was generally a beautiful turquoise but here the water was more of an inky blue. Could it be the shipwreck that was causing this he wondered. Certainly the bluish patch didn't look unlike the shape of a ship! He decided to take out his binoculars and have a closer look at it . . .

Use your BINOCULARS CARD to obtain a clearer view of this patch of sea yourself by placing it exactly over the shape below – then follow the instruction. If you don't have a BINOCULARS CARD in your AIRCRAFT CARD, go to 278 instead.

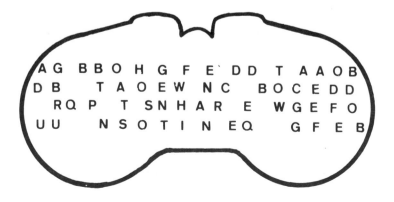

146

'Well, well, well!' Bertie exclaimed as he decoded the symbols on the camera. 'Listen to this – *PROVISIONED TO SECRET AGENT WERNER WOLFF*. This is obviously the camera he was given when he worked for that enemy intelligence service. It looks like the blueprints weren't the only thing the old devil absconded with!' As the trio continued towards the marsh, they wondered what the camera was doing there. 'Presumably it was the one Wolff used to photograph the flamingos,' Biggles said. 'After removing the finished film, he probably decided it would be best to get rid of it.' *Go to 50.*

147

'There she is, old boy!' Bertie suddenly exclaimed as he found the waterfall with his binoculars. 'About three miles to our right. You can just see its spray steaming up above the trees. There's obviously quite some force behind it!' *Go to 153.*

148

Biggles doubted whether consulting the map would be of much use to them, however. 'Even if your map *does* give the depth of the lagoon,' he told Ginger, 'we can't be sure that the water level doesn't change with the seasons. In a very dry period, like it is now, the water could be much shallower.' He thought for a moment. 'No, I think the best thing we can do is dive as close to the lagoon as possible and see how it looks.' So that is what they did, coming to the decision that the water probably *was* deep enough for a landing. And so it proved . . . for a few minutes later the Auster was floating happily on the surface of the lagoon! **Go to 160.**

149

Ginger immediately returned his binoculars to their case, however. This was silly, he told himself – he was letting the islanders' superstitions about the wreck get to him. How could there be anyone on board? It was probably just a large sea-bird he had seen! **Go to 66.**

150

'Do you think the blueprints *are* going to be at the end of these seventy paces?' Bertie asked, breathless with anticipation, as they followed the direction Ginger's compass was pointing – due south. He soon had his answer. For just short of their seventieth pace, they came across a large iron box, submerged in the marshy water. They yanked it up and hurriedly carried it to drier ground. 'Please don't let it be locked!' Ginger implored as Biggles prepared to prise open the lid. Ginger's prayers were answered – the box wasn't locked. And the prayers of all the team were answered – for there, hidden inside, were the missing blueprints!

You have successfully completed the mission! Well done.

151

'Don't tell me you *have* spotted something, old boy!' Bertie exclaimed as Ginger's brow suddenly took on a thoughtful frown. 'Well, what is it for Pete's sake? All I can see down there where you're looking is a sandy beach with a fallen palm-tree!' But it was precisely this fallen palm-tree that so interested Ginger. With its splayed branches, it looked just like an arrow! 'Maybe the tree was felled by Wolff, not by the wind!' Ginger suggested excitedly. 'It could be to show which direction one has to fly across Flamingo Island for the blueprints. I'm going to take out my compass!'

Use your COMPASS CARD to find which direction the fallen palm-tree is indicating by placing it exactly over the shape below – and with the pointer touching north. Then go to the number that appears in the window. If you don't have a COMPASS CARD, you'll have to guess which of the numbers to go to.

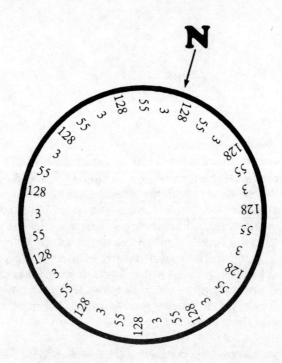

Biggles told Ginger there was no need for his map, however. 'I remember seeing that old harbour on the map of the island we were shown back in Jamaica,' he said. 'It's not that difficult to remember. The harbour was one of the few man-made features on the island! It's situated in the north-east corner.' As the old harbour now disappeared behind them, Biggles made a quick check of his fuel gauge. All those miles they had flown from Jamaica meant that it was down a quarter already.

Move the pointer on your FUEL GAUGE one coloured segment clockwise. Now go to 236.

The Auster was soon circling over the waterfall, Biggles looking to see if it were possible to land nearby. Fortunately, it was – because a river started at the base of the waterfall, a river that quickly became quite wide. 'I'll bring her down about a mile away from the falls,' Biggles said as he gently pushed on the control column. 'I daren't make it any nearer in case the river's flowing too fast.' *Go to 90.*

The description that the boy gave of the man fitted Wolff perfectly: round glasses and a blond moustache! But what excited the team even more was a question the man had apparently asked the boy. 'He wanted to know if there was any part of the island that I was afraid of,' the boy said. 'I told him the wrecked ship. I told him everyone on the island was. I told him there were evil spirits there and no one ever goes near it!' The trio immediately thanked the boy and hurried back to their plane. They were all convinced this wrecked ship was where the blueprints were hidden!

Throw the SPECIAL DICE to determine who is to reach the Auster first.

BIGGLES thrown	go to 271
BERTIE thrown	go to 238
GINGER thrown	go to 83

155

As Ginger was unfolding his map, however, he realised he didn't really want the marsh to be large enough to be shown. The bigger it was, the longer it would take to search it for clues! ***Go to 219.***

156

'By Jove, Biggles, you're right!' Bertie exclaimed as they moved a few hundred metres nearer the small hazy shape. 'It is a hut! Maybe Wolff sheltered in there for a while. It did look pretty stormy on that photograph of his. Come on,' he enthused, breaking into a run, 'I think we should investigate it right away!'

Throw the SPECIAL DICE to determine who is to reach the hut first.

BIGGLES thrown	go to 212
BERTIE thrown	go to 11
GINGER thrown	go to 39

157

'The rocks are pointing in a north-westerly direction!' Ginger said excitedly when he had read his compass. So Biggles immediately turned the Auster north-westwards, depressing his left rudder pedal. Of course, it might have been mere chance that the rocks had been in the shape of an arrow. And even if it wasn't, there was nothing to say that Wolff was the person responsible for arranging them in that way. But when one was as desperate for clues as Biggles and his team were, objections like those were conveniently ignored! ***Go to 215.***

158

The team had flown a good ten miles or so over the island when Ginger suddenly gave an excited cry. 'What is it, old boy?' Bertie asked eagerly. 'Have you spotted something important? All I can see down there is a banana plantation!' But that was exactly what had so delighted Ginger. He had never seen a banana tree before! 'It will also help us find exactly where we are on the island,' he said, reaching into his jacket pocket for his map.

Use your MAP to find which square the banana plantation is in – then follow the instruction. If you don't have a MAP in your AIRCRAFT CARD, you'll have to guess which instruction to follow.

If you think E3	go to 91
If you think E4	go to 173
If you think D3	go to 214

159

'Can't see anything!' Ginger remarked as they all surveyed the dunes through their binoculars. 'Hang on a minute, though,' he suddenly added excitedly, 'I think I can see something glinting in the sun!' When the others had located it too, Biggles immediately took the Auster as close as he could to the shore. Ginger leapt out into the shallows and splashed towards the spot he had pointed out. 'It's a compass!' he told them eagerly on his return. 'And, look, there's a name engraved on the back. The name of Werner Wolff!'

If you don't already have it there, put the COMPASS CARD into your AIRCRAFT CARD. Now go to 236.

'Well, it looks as if we made that landing and long walk for nothing!' Ginger sighed when they had reached the collection of huts. 'There's not a soul around!' They were just about to return to their plane, however, when Bertie noticed some strange symbols chalked on one of the hut doors. 'It looks distinctly like a coded message!' he remarked, immediately reaching into his inside pocket for his copy of Wolff's codebook. 'Maybe this trek wasn't for nothing after all!'

Use your CODEBOOK CARD to find out what the symbols mean by decoding the instruction below. If you don't have a CODEBOOK CARD in your AIRCRAFT CARD, go to 46 instead.

'Yes, there is someone there!' Biggles exclaimed with alarm as he focused his binoculars on the distant aircraft. 'And I think he's more than just a curious islander. The figure's acting much too suspiciously. Come on, let's get down there as quickly as possible!' *Go to 142.*

The team had flown only another ten miles or so from the mountain when they reached the sea again. 'I wonder which part this is?' Biggles asked as he banked the Auster to the left to obtain a better view. 'The coastline is certainly a lot more treacherous here. Look at the steep cliffs, and those three jagged rocks sticking out of the water. They would tear a ship to pieces!' Since the rocks were of a fair size, he asked Ginger to see if they were shown on his map.

Use your MAP to find which square the three jagged rocks are in – then follow the instruction. If you don't have a MAP in your AIRCRAFT CARD, you'll have to guess which instruction to follow.

If you think A2	go to 137
If you think A1	go to 21
If you think B1	go to 82

163

Before Ginger had time to open out his map, however, the Auster had touched down on the river. It seemed there weren't any hidden rocks there, after all! Biggles took the plane as near to the bank as he dared, and then checked the fuel gauge before he switched off the engine. The pointer had dropped a bit since he'd last looked!

Move the pointer on your FUEL GAUGE one coloured segment clockwise. Now go to 109. (Remember: when the pointer reaches the DANGER segment on your FUEL GAUGE, you must immediately stop the game and start all over again from the beginning.)

164

As soon as they had moored the plane securely – they didn't want it floating down to the sea! – the trio started the two or so mile trek back to the marsh. They must have been about halfway there when Bertie spotted something on the ground. It was a gun! Picking it up – very carefully in case it were loaded – he saw that there were what looked like symbols of a code engraved along the barrel. He immediately reached into his jacket pocket for his copy of Wolff's codebook.

Use your CODEBOOK CARD to find out what the symbols mean by decoding the instruction below. If you don't have a CODEBOOK CARD in your AIRCRAFT CARD, go to 95 instead.

165

'What an absolute fiend that Wolff was!' Bertie remarked when he had decoded the message scratched on the flask. 'This says: *THE WHISKY INSIDE IS LACED WITH A DEADLY POISON!* Wolff obviously meant to offer it to anyone who was proving a nuisance.' Ginger came to Wolff's defence, though, asking what proof there was that the flask was his. 'These initials on the stopper, old boy,' Bertie replied rather smugly, adjusting his monocle. 'Look – *W.W.*!' *Go to 89.*

166

The woman put her hand on Ginger's arm, though, to let him know that he didn't need his map. She obviously took more of a liking to him than she did to Bertie! 'The waterfall's over there,' she told him, pointing into the distance. 'You will see it very easily when you are up in the sky.' The trio thanked the woman, quickly climbing back into their plane. They were sure the waterfall was where Wolff had hidden the blueprints! *Go to 197.*

167

'I wonder if it's been washed up from the wreck?' Ginger asked as he strolled over to the iron box. Then an even more exciting thought occurred to him. Might it contain the blueprints? Opening the rusty lid, however, he found that the box was completely empty. He was just about to let the lid drop shut again when he noticed a tiny message scratched into the metal. It read: *BLUE-PRINTS FOUR HUNDRED AND FIFTY METRES SOUTH-WEST*. He immediately reached into his jacket pocket for his compass!

Use your COMPASS CARD to find south-west by placing it

exactly over the shape below – and with the pointer touching
north. Then go to the number that appears in the window. If you
don't have a COMPASS CARD, you'll have to guess which of
the numbers to go to.

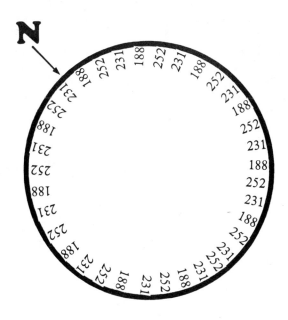

'Hey, I think I might have found something myself!' Biggles
suddenly remarked. He pointed down to the turquoise shallows at
the western edge of the isle. 'That's a buoy bobbing up and down,
isn't it? Maybe Wolff hid the blueprints under the water – in a bottle
or something – and the buoy is marking their position!' Since

Biggles couldn't see any rocks near the buoy, he decided to bring the plane down so that they could have a closer look. 'Perfect!' Bertie complimented him as the Auster skated to a halt only metres from the bright orange buoy. 'And it looks as if you might well be right about it being connected with Wolff!' he said excitedly as the buoy ducked and jumped in the swell they had created. 'I can see some symbols on it. Maybe it's a coded message. Now where's my copy of Wolff's codebook!'

Use your CODEBOOK CARD to find out what the symbols mean by decoding the instruction below. If you don't have a CODEBOOK CARD in your AIRCRAFT CARD, go to 16 instead.

Biggles had foolishly put the scrap of paper on the sand while he took out his codebook . . . foolishly because there was quite a wind blowing across the beach. Suddenly, it whisked the paper into the air, not dropping it again until it was way out over the sea. 'Well, let's just hope it had nothing to do with Wolff!' Biggles said, annoyed with himself, as they boarded the plane again. Just before taking off, Biggles checked the fuel gauge. They were down to three-quarters of a tank.

Move the pointer on your FUEL GAUGE one coloured segment clockwise. Now go to 236.

Biggles told Bertie and Ginger not to bother with their binoculars, though. He would only have to keep circling round while they looked through them, and it would be just as quick for him to swoop down towards the orange shape. So that's exactly what he did, pushing on the control column. 'Well, there's your life-jacket, I'm afraid, Ginger,' Biggles said as they passed within twenty metres of the object. 'It's just a large plastic tray! It probably belongs to one of the island's inhabitants – used for collecting crabs or something.' As the Auster now climbed into the air again, Biggles checked the fuel gauge. It was down a quarter!

Move the pointer on your FUEL GAUGE one coloured segment clockwise. Now go to 4.

'Just fly across the caves once more, will you, old boy?' Bertie asked eagerly on their third swoop past. 'I'm sure I saw what looked like a large greenish arrow above one of them!' So Biggles turned the Auster round, pushing the control column sharply forward again. 'See it!' Bertie exclaimed a few seconds later. 'Above the cave on the left, about a metre long! Now it's my bet that Wolff painted it there to indicate which direction to fly across the island!' Ginger obviously thought the same because he was already digging into his jacket pocket for his compass . . .

Use your COMPASS CARD to find which direction the arrow is indicating by placing it exactly over the shape below – and with the pointer touching north. Then go to the number that appears in the window. If you don't have a COMPASS CARD, you'll have to guess which of the numbers to go to.

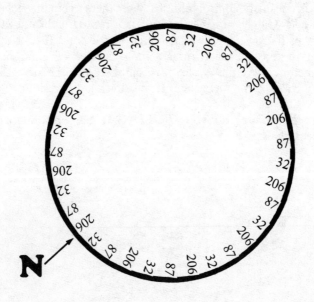

172

'The old fellow's pointing slightly south-west from here,' Biggles told the others as he consulted his compass. 'I'm by no means convinced that he really understood our question but we might as well try flying in that direction anyway. You never know!' So the trio waved the old man goodbye and started their journey back towards the Auster. They hadn't walked very far when Ginger noticed a faded map on the ground. Perhaps Wolff had been in this vicinity after all!

If you don't already have it there, put the MAP into your AIRCRAFT CARD. Now go to 106.

173

The team had now spent a good hour flying over the island, first northwards and then to the west, and they still hadn't spotted anything significant. But then Ginger looked at the craggy, bluish mountain that was looming up ahead of them. There was a wooden cross on top, presumably denoting that this was the highest point on the island. 'If I was wanting a hiding-place,' he announced with sudden excitement, 'I think I might well choose right up there!' **Go to 232.**

174

Just as Biggles was about to consult his compass, they all heard a noise way over to their left. They immediately started to run in that direction. The noise sounded very much like an aircraft's engine being warmed up – an *Auster*'s engine! 'Someone must be trying to steal her,' Ginger said with alarm as they went. 'Let's hope we make it in time or we'll be stranded on this island!' **Go to 98.**

175

'What did this man look like?' Biggles asked eagerly. 'Did he have round glasses and a blond moustache?' When the woman nodded her head, he excitedly asked the next question – where *was* the waterfall? 'Over that way!' she answered, pointing into the distance. 'Many miles in that direction!' Biggles immediately dug into his pockets for his compass, so he could check the direction the woman was pointing.

Use your COMPASS CARD to find this direction yourself by placing it exactly over the shape below – and with the pointer touching north. Then go to the number that appears in the window. If you don't have a COMPASS CARD, you'll have to guess which of the numbers to go to.

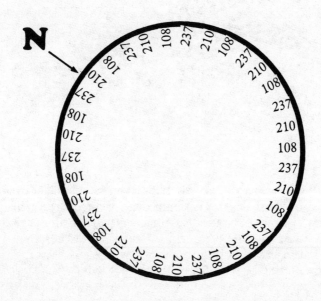

176

The huge rock *was* shown on Ginger's map. It was in the south-west corner of the island. 'I wonder how it got there?' Ginger asked as the coastline now turned sharply northwards, Biggles banking the plane accordingly. 'The rest of the bay just looks like very fine grains of sand. The rock seems most out of place!' He shrugged his shoulders as he returned his map to his pocket. 'Still, I suppose geology has produced some even odder sights!' ***Go to 145.***

177

Bertie was the first to reach the part of the beach directly opposite the shipwreck, although the others arrived very soon after him. 'It's a smallish schooner,' Biggles remarked as they squinted across the four hundred or so metres of water. 'A two-mast type. It must have been sitting there for about fifty years, by the look of it.' Ginger was just moving to his right a little to observe the wreck from a different angle when his foot struck a metal tube embedded in the sand. 'It seems to be a container of some sort,' he said, noticing the screw-on

lid at one end. 'And look, there's a coded inscription down the side!'
He immediately reached into his pocket for his copy of Wolff's
codebook.

*Use your **CODEBOOK CARD** to find out what the inscription
means by decoding the instruction below. If you don't have a
CODEBOOK CARD in your **AIRCRAFT CARD**, go to 274
instead.*

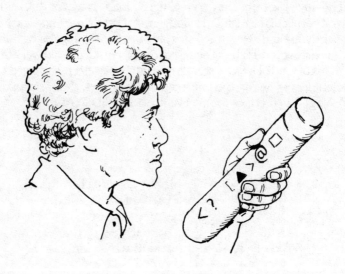

178

'It looks as if it might be OK down there,' Biggles said, pointing
down to his right after they had flown several miles along the coast
of the island. In actual fact, the bay he had pointed out didn't belong
to the island at all but to a little offshoot from it, separated by half a

mile of sea. This tiny islet was shaped roughly like a key and Biggles was rather hoping that it might prove a key in more ways than one! As the Auster started its descent to the bay, Bertie thought he would look for the key-shaped isle on his map. It would show their exact position.

Use your MAP to find which square the key-shaped isle is in – then follow the instruction. If you don't have a MAP in your AIRCRAFT CARD, you'll have to guess which instruction to follow.

If you think D1	go to 44
If you think E1	go to 140
If you think E2	go to 251

179

Biggles said they were likely to be much more successful if they actually *walked* along the beach, however. So Bertie left his binoculars in their case while Biggles gently taxied the Auster towards the sand. They searched the dunes for a good hour – but they didn't find so much as a cigarette butt! 'Oh well,' Biggles sighed as they all returned to the Auster's cockpit, 'perhaps we'll have more luck flying *across* the island!' **Go to 236.**

'The old boy's telescope is pointing virtually due north,' Bertie told the others when he had consulted his compass. 'That's the way I reckon we should fly!' Biggles was far from convinced by Bertie's theory about why the admiral's statue was pointing inland. But then north seemed as good a direction to fly as any other! *Go to 103.*

'The patch of water nearest to the village, as far as I can see,' Bertie said, pointing down to Biggles' left, 'is that lagoon. It would mean a bit of a hike for us – but only a couple of miles or so.' So Biggles guided the Auster down on to the lagoon, the water surging up from its floats. 'Don't stop just yet!' Bertie suddenly cried as Biggles was about to switch off the engine. 'There's a piece of wood floating on the water a few metres ahead of us and there are some strange symbols painted on it. I'm sure it's a coded message!' He quickly reached into his pocket for his copy of Wolff's codebook while Biggles moved the plane forward a little.

Use your CODEBOOK CARD to find out what the message says by decoding the instruction below. If you don't have a CODEBOOK CARD in your AIRCRAFT CARD, go to 93 instead.

'I'd better get myself a new monocle!' Bertie exclaimed as he focused his binoculars on the lake. 'There's our Auster, as clear as day!' So with considerable relief, they now made their way back towards the plane – the climb down fortunately proving a lot quicker than the climb up. 'I'm afraid that was one big waste of time!' Ginger apologised as they finally took to the air again. *Go to 162.*

Biggles kept circling the plane over the clearing while Bertie focused his binoculars on the bundle. 'Well, is it a parachute or isn't it?' Ginger asked impatiently. 'If it is, then there's a chance that Wolff might have dropped a notebook or something nearby! Our search could soon be over . . .' But Bertie stopped Ginger short with the bad news. 'I'm afraid it's *not* a parachute, old boy,' he said with a little embarrassment. 'Those trees down there are banana trees. And that yellow bundle is just a bunch of the blessed things that has fallen off!' *Go to 48.*

'Well, anywhere on the right bank, old boy!' Bertie suggested. 'That's the side the marsh is on. We don't want to alight on the left bank or we'll have to find somewhere to cross the river!' As Biggles aimed the Auster for near the right bank, pushing on the control column, Ginger thought he would look for the estuary of the river on his map. He just wanted to make sure there weren't any hidden rocks they should avoid!

Use your MAP to find which square the river joins the sea – then follow the instruction. If you don't have a MAP in your AIRCRAFT CARD, you'll have to guess which instruction to follow.

If you think C4	go to 84
If you think B4	go to 163
If you think A4	go to 109

185

Ginger was still trying to find the wrecked ship on his map when Biggles returned to the plane and slid into his seat at the controls. 'Sorry about that,' he said, immediately starting the engine, 'but I suddenly realised that the boy hadn't told us where the shipwreck was. The poor chap was rather reluctant to tell me at first, begging me not to go anywhere near the place, but he eventually spilt the beans. Mind you,' he added with a chuckle, 'it cost me my compass as a bribe!'

If you have it there, remove the COMPASS CARD from your AIRCRAFT CARD. Now go to 86.

The Auster now passed directly over the shipwreck. 'I don't want to put down too near it,' Biggles said thoughtfully as he examined the colour of the water beyond for a safe bright blue area. 'Presumably, the ship sank because there are some hidden rocks there. We don't want to fall foul of them ourselves!' He shielded his eyes against the sea's glare for a moment. 'Look, that seems a good spot,' he said, starting to push on the control column to bring the plane down. 'About three-quarters of a mile further along the bay!' *Go to 123.*

'Our brains must have rusted!' Biggles told the others eagerly. 'Where should we have gone first on our search? The precise spot where the photograph of the flamingo was taken, of course – the marsh! I'm not promising that this is where the blueprints are actually hidden but at least we know for sure that Wolff did visit it. And he might have dropped some vital clues there!' Bertie and Ginger immediately became more enthusiastic, sharing Biggles' theory about the marsh. All they had to do now was work out in which direction it lay!

Throw the SPECIAL DICE to determine who is to provide the answer.

BIGGLES thrown	go to 259
BERTIE thrown	go to 133
GINGER thrown	go to 36

188

Bertie told Ginger he didn't need to consult his compass, though. 'Think about it, old chap,' he said eagerly. 'Four hundred and fifty metres . . . that's just about how far out the wreck is. Surely the message must be directing us to that. You can take for granted that it's south-west!' *Go to 264.*

189

'Here we are!' Bertie declared, pleased with himself, as he found the bottle-shaped islet on his map. 'It's just off the south-east tip of Flamingo Island. Rum-Bottle Island it's called. I dare say it was pirates who gave it that name! You can just picture them on a place like that, can't you?' As the others peered ahead at the empty white beaches, the waving palms, the secret creeks, they found themselves agreeing with Bertie. Yes, they *could* just picture pirates there! *Go to 275.*

190

'Couldn't have done it better myself, old chap!' Bertie praised Biggles as the Auster skimmed along the water, having made a perfect landing on the bay. 'But I don't know what good it's going to do us, I'm sure! Staring at those blessed sand-dunes certainly doesn't give *me* any inspiration!' But Biggles remained optimistic, saying they might spot something that Wolff had dropped on the beach. Even his discarded water-bottle – though not a secret blueprint – would at least confirm that Flamingo Island was definitely the right place. 'I see your point, old chap,' Bertie considered more enthusiastically. 'Let's take a squint at the beach through our binoculars!'

Use your BINOCULARS CARD to obtain a clearer view of the beach by placing it exactly over the shape below – then follow the instruction. If you don't have a BINOCULARS CARD in your AIRCRAFT CARD, go to 179 instead.

'Our dear old friend is a bit of a practical joker, I'm afraid!' Bertie remarked with a huff when he had used his codebook to work out the symbols Ginger had scribbled down. 'His message translates as: *YOU DIDN'T REALLY THINK THE SEARCH WOULD BE THIS EASY DID YOU? YOU'VE A LOT MORE MILES*

TO TRAVEL YET!' Biggles was the only one of the three who didn't seem infuriated by the message. 'Well, at least it definitely proves that Wolff did come to this island!' he pointed out. **Go to 218.**

192

Ginger led the trek towards the base of the mountain, marching so eagerly that the others could barely keep up! But an hour or so later, the climb having become much steeper, he started to tire. 'How much *further* to the top, for goodness' sake?' he asked wearily. 'This mountain is higher than it looks!' It was then that Biggles remembered he had a map with him. That should show the height of the mountain!

Use your MAP to find which square the mountain with the cross is in – then follow the instruction. If you don't have a MAP in your AIRCRAFT CARD, you'll have to guess which instruction to follow.

If you think B1	go to 244
If you think C1	go to 268
If you think C2	go to 208

Just as Biggles was opening his map, however, he suddenly started. 'What is it, old chap?' Bertie asked with concern. But Biggles, who immediately dashed off towards the bay, had no time to answer. He'd heard a lot of birds squawking from that direction and was worried that there might be someone snooping round their plane. 'False alarm, thank goodness!' he said to the others when they had caught up with him at the Auster. 'I thought we might have unwelcome visitors!' *Was* it a false alarm, though? Biggles was sure he had left his binoculars in the plane but they were now nowhere to be found!

If you have it there, remove the BINOCULARS CARD from your AIRCRAFT CARD. Now go to 106.

194

The trio at last reached the bottom of the mountain again. But which way was their plane? The Auster had been constantly in view further up but now it was obscured by a mass of trees! 'You two forgot that we wouldn't always be able to see over the treetops, didn't you?' Biggles chuckled. 'Well, it's a good job one of us realised. When we were at the top, I checked the Auster's direction on my compass. It's north-west of the mountain!' Biggles now took his compass out again so he could find north-west.

Use your COMPASS CARD to find north-west yourself by

placing it exactly over the shape below – and with the pointer touching north. Then go to the number that appears in the window. If you don't have a COMPASS CARD, you'll have to guess which of the numbers to go to.

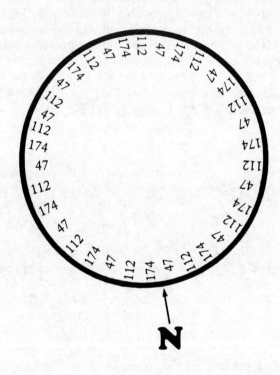

'We're just north of the centre of the island,' Ginger informed Biggles when he had located the sugar plantation on his map. As he folded the map up again, he asked if either of them knew the purpose of the kilns. 'I can only guess that they were for boiling the cane extracts,' Biggles replied, rather unsure himself. 'Presumably the stuff had to be heated before sugar was produced.' **Go to 48.**

196

'Sorry for doubting you, Biggles, old chap,' Bertie apologised when he had focused his binoculars on the birds. 'They *are* flamingos, after all. I'm obviously not the sharp bird-spotter I thought I was!' It wasn't much longer before the flamingos started to land . . . and Biggles was right, their destination was the marsh! **Go to 261.**

197

The team had been in the air for a good ten minutes since leaving the woman but still they couldn't spot the waterfall. They were beginning to wonder if she had deliberately sent them up the garden path! 'I can't see it *anywhere*,' Biggles said, bewildered, as he banked the plane to left and right. 'Have a squint through your binoculars, Bertie!'

Use your BINOCULARS CARD to try and spot the waterfall by placing it exactly over the shape below – then follow the instruction. If you don't have a BINOCULARS CARD in your AIRCRAFT CARD, go to 24 instead.

```
S G P P R O M L M S   U U S     T P P O S
P T R     W P O   L R L N X E   Z R S     T R Z
  F N I T     O U T N T E K K U  L S L     R
P  M S Q I P E  Q Q  V T X   E V V X N   T
```

198

Training his binoculars on the turquoise water, Bertie suddenly spotted the wrecked ship. 'It's about a mile ahead of us,' he told the others excitedly, 'four hundred metres or so from the shore. You can't miss it – at least half of it is sticking out of the water!' ***Go to 186.***

199

Ginger's map *did* show the shipwreck – and it did give the date the tragedy occurred: 1937! 'It's apparently been sitting there for quite some time,' Ginger told the others as they joined him. 'I just hope the schooner was carrying cargo, not passengers. The death toll wouldn't have been as high!' But Biggles very much doubted that there had been a death toll at all. The schooner was so close to the shore that, unless there had been an almighty storm, the people on board could probably have swum to safety. ***Go to 264.***

200

Biggles stepped on to the bank first, the others only seconds behind! And they immediately started to follow the river upstream, towards the waterfall. As they were walking, Bertie suddenly noticed a small rusty object on the ground. It was rectangular with a stopper at one end. 'Looks like someone's hip-flask!' he exclaimed as he examined it. 'You know – for holding brandy and the like. Hey, what do we have here, scratched down the side? I do believe it's some sort of coded message!' He quickly reached into his inside pocket for his copy of Wolff's codebook . . .

Use your CODEBOOK CARD to find out what the message says by decoding the instruction below. If you don't have a CODEBOOK CARD in your AIRCRAFT CARD, go to 211 instead.

201

Biggles now navigated the Auster slowly towards the beach. 'Nice to stretch the old legs!' Bertie remarked as they all jumped out on to the white sand. They weren't really *expecting* to find anything on the beach but they strolled along, keeping their eyes on the ground. Wolff might possibly have dropped something that they could identify as belonging to him. It would hardly be the blueprints but at least it would confirm that he had definitely visited the area! *Go to 92.*

The trio had only measured out thirty of the paces due south when a gunshot rang out across the marsh. At first they thought it was just a flamingo hunter but when further shots came, passing uncomfortably close to them, they realised it was a different story. *They* were the target . . . and it wasn't just one gunman, there were several! 'They must be crouched in the reeds somewhere!' Biggles exclaimed, desperately looking round. 'We've obviously been followed here by another team interested in the blueprints. Well, we clearly can't stay here. Our priority must be our safety and so we'll try and make a run for it back to the Auster. We'll return to this island some other time . . . when we're suitably armed!'

Your mission wasn't successful, unfortunately. If you would like another attempt at it, you must start the game all over again from the beginning. Try setting off with a different EQUIPMENT CARD this time to see if it gives you any more luck!

Just as Bertie was taking his map from his jacket pocket, however, a most beautiful sight appeared before their eyes. A bright pink cloud rose from the island. Flamingos! Hundreds of them! 'Well, I think that saves you the bother of consulting your map, Bertie!' Biggles chuckled as he watched the cloud swirl round before drifting down again. 'There can surely be no doubt now that that's Flamingo Island!' Returning the map to his pocket, Bertie suddenly realised his compass wasn't there. 'Blast!' he exclaimed when he found it wasn't on the floor of the plane either. 'I must have dropped it before we left Jamaica!'

If you have it there, remove the COMPASS CARD from your AIRCRAFT CARD. Now go to 275.

204

By the time Ginger was ready with his compass, however, the island had become much clearer. Its green shape now stood out quite vividly from the haze. So Ginger decided to return the compass to his jacket pocket but as he did so he noticed that his copy of Wolff's codebook was missing! 'Don't look so alarmed about it, old boy!' Bertie chuckled. 'I'm sure someone hasn't lifted it from your pocket, if that's what you're thinking. It probably just fell out somewhere back in Jamaica!' Ginger smiled, pretending to agree with Bertie. But deep down he remained uneasy. He'd always been careful to keep that pocket securely zipped!

If you have it there, remove the CODEBOOK CARD from your AIRCRAFT CARD. Now go to 256.

205

As they slowly approached the shore of Flamingo Island, Bertie decided to have another look at that photograph of Wolff's and reached into his inside pocket for it. Maybe there was *another* clue there, one that they hadn't noticed before. 'No . . . one silly flamingo and a few reeds!' he tutted – but then he spotted what looked like minute symbols at the bottom of the photograph. Were they some form of coded message? He quickly searched his pockets for his copy of Wolff's codebook!

Use your CODEBOOK CARD to find out what the symbols

mean by decoding the instruction below. If you don't have a
CODEBOOK CARD in your **AIRCRAFT CARD**, go to 116
instead.

206

The Auster now left the caves behind, venturing inland. There
began a floor of dense vegetation, dark and sinister. 'We're going to
have to keep a watchful eye on our juice,' Biggles said after several
miles of the monotonous scene. 'I hardly think we're going to find
somewhere to refuel in a place like this!' He decided to quickly
check the fuel gauge right now. It was down a little since he'd last
looked!

*Move the pointer on your FUEL GAUGE one coloured
segment clockwise. Now go to 269.*

Ginger's map showed two large caves in the south-east corner of the island. He quickly checked to see if there was another pair of caves anywhere else on the map. There wasn't, so he decided that they must be at the south-east corner! **Go to 246.**

The trio finally reached the wooden cross at the top of the mountain. But if the blueprints *were* hidden up there, there was certainly little evidence of them. No secret cavities gouged into the cross, or signs of digging nearby! The team were just having a brief rest before their return down the mountain when Bertie gave a cry of concern. He could no longer make out their aircraft at the end of the lake! 'I know it's quite a way off,' he said anxiously, quickly unstrapping his binoculars case, 'but surely we should at least be able to see a dot?'

Use your BINOCULARS CARD to obtain a clearer view of the lake by placing it exactly over the shape below – then follow the instruction. If you don't have a BINOCULARS CARD in your AIRCRAFT CARD, go to 34 instead.

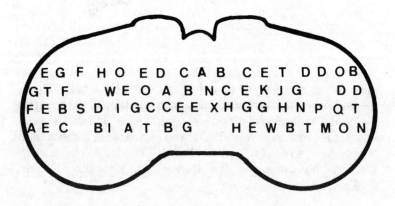

By the time Bertie was ready with his binoculars, however, the Auster had moved a lot closer to the birds. Their curved necks and pink plumage were now quite unmistakable. They *were* flamingos after all! 'Look, they're starting to land,' Biggles said, his eyes carefully following their descent. 'Now, is that the marsh down there? Yes, by Jove, it is!' It was with some relief that Biggles spotted this swamped ground, for he had just noticed his fuel gauge. It had dropped quite a bit since his last check!

Move the pointer on your FUEL GAUGE one coloured segment clockwise. Now go to 261.

210

The trio bade the woman goodbye and climbed back into their plane so they could set off in the direction she had shown them. As they were flying, Ginger thought he would try and find the waterfall on his map. It might give an idea as to how big it was!

Use your MAP to find which square the waterfall is in – then follow the instruction. If you don't have a MAP in your AIRCRAFT CARD, you'll have to guess which instruction to follow.

If you think C2	go to 153
If you think B2	go to 110
If you think B3	go to 222

211

Biggles told Bertie that they could work out the coded message on the hip-flask later, however. Their priority had to be exploring the waterfall! Biggles was in such a hurry to lead them along the river-bank, though, that he suddenly slipped on the muddy ground. His compass fell from his pocket as he did so and rolled into the murky water. 'Not much chance of finding that again, old boy!' Bertie told him with a sigh as he helped him to his feet.

If you have it there, remove the COMPASS CARD from your AIRCRAFT CARD. Now go to 89.

212

Biggles just reached the hut first, pushing through the palm-leaf door. In fact, the whole thing seemed to be made of woven palm-leaves – the roof, walls and floor! 'It seems to have been some sort of observation hut,' Biggles told the others as they now joined him inside the dilapidated structure. 'To watch the flamingos, presumably. Look, you can see hundreds of them from this small window!' As they watched the birds for a few moments, Ginger noticed that one of them never seemed to move. 'Let me get out my binoculars,' he suggested thoughtfully. 'I'm sure that's not really a flamingo at all!'

Use your BINOCULARS CARD to obtain a clearer view of the

flamingo by placing it exactly over the shape below – then follow the instruction. If you don't have a BINOCULARS CARD in your AIRCRAFT CARD, go to 51 instead.

D G B A O C C F L K F H F T D B B O A
  T E   D W   O   C C   R N G H   E C D
        N P   T   R H U R S E E W F F H O
P E S T U I Z   G S   H R W E T F O G

213

While Bertie was searching his jacket pockets for his compass, Biggles decided to take a closer look at the statue, pushing on the control column. 'I'm afraid you've let your imagination run away with you, Bertie,' he told him with a chuckle as he flew as near to the top of the stone admiral as he dared. 'It would require a good half-dozen men to shift a weight like that. Wolff on his own couldn't possibly have done it!' As Biggles picked up height again, he glanced at the fuel gauge. Those fifty miles from Jamaica meant that they were down a quarter of a tank already!

Move the pointer on your FUEL GAUGE one coloured segment clockwise. Now go to 103.

214

Ginger's map showed that the banana plantation was in the south-east of the island, about a dozen miles below and to the right of its centre. 'I wonder if the plantation's still in use,' Biggles pondered as they continued flying over it. 'If it is, then maybe there's someone there who actually *met* Wolff.' But the plantation had a decidedly abandoned look to it – with not a picker or vehicle in sight! *Go to 173.*

215

The Auster had still to reach Flamingo Island when Biggles thought he saw a tiny flash of light high up above them. Was it another aircraft, its wings briefly reflecting the sun? He grew a little uneasy. Maybe they were being followed! But perhaps it wasn't a plane, after all . . . just his imagination. To find out, he asked Ginger if he would search that part of the sky through his binoculars.

Use your BINOCULARS CARD to obtain a closer view of the sky by placing it exactly over the shape below – then follow the instruction. If you don't have a BINOCULARS CARD in your AIRCRAFT CARD, go to 102 instead.

216

It was Biggles who spotted some evidence. Evidence that Wolff had definitely *not* visited the caves rather than that he had! 'Our friend couldn't possibly have come here to hide the blueprints,' Biggles said as he flew alongside the caves once more. 'Look how dangerous that sea is. There's simply no way you could navigate a boat there! And the cliffs are far too steep to attempt a descent.' As Biggles now turned the Auster inland, Ginger decided to look for the caves on his map. It would tell them precisely in which part of the island they were.

Use your MAP to find which square the caves are in – then follow the instruction. If you don't have a MAP in your AIRCRAFT CARD, you'll have to guess which instruction to follow.

If you think E3   go to 207
If you think E2   go to 276
If you think E1   go to 246

217

'The map gives the lagoon's depth as eight metres in the centre and two metres at the edge,' Ginger was soon informing his skipper. 'So as long as this island hasn't had a very dry period, and the water-level hasn't dropped a lot, it should be perfectly all right for a landing!' So Biggles guided the Auster towards the lagoon, aiming for as near to its edge as he dared. 'Only a bit of a paddle for you!' he joked as the plane came to a stop just short of the reeds. *Go to 160.*

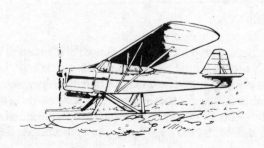

Biggles was just about to leave the caves and turn inland when a thought suddenly occurred to him. Having learnt that Wolff's message was a joke, they had all assumed that the caves obviously weren't his hiding-place after all. But why not? Maybe it was a double-bluff by Wolff! 'At the very least, we ought to give the caves another look,' Biggles told the others. As he prepared the plane for another dive towards the caves, he asked Bertie and Ginger to get out their binoculars. 'I'll fly as close to them as I can so that you can get a good look inside,' he said.

*Use your **BINOCULARS CARD** to obtain a clearer view of the inside of the caves by placing it exactly over the shape below – then follow the instruction. If you don't have a **BINOCULARS CARD** in your **AIRCRAFT CARD**, go to 277 instead.*

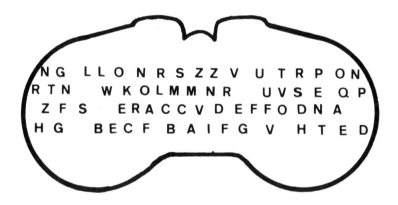

Ginger was still trying to find the marsh on his map when Biggles suddenly spotted it a few miles over to their left. 'Gosh, there must be well over a hundred flamingos down there!' he remarked as he flew nearer, trying to work out whether they could land on the flooded ground. The flamingos in the centre seemed to be standing in quite a lot of water and so he decided they probably could! As Biggles manoeuvred the plane for the landing, he happened to glance at the fuel gauge. The pointer had dropped quite a bit since his last look.

Move the pointer on your FUEL GAUGE one coloured segment clockwise. Now go to 94.

220

'There's no need to bother with your binoculars, Ginger,' Biggles told him over his shoulder. 'I'll swoop down over the pier so you can take a better look at it.' He immediately pushed on the control column and the plane dived to within ten metres of the pier. 'It doesn't seem so bad close to,' Ginger said as they swept up into the air again. 'I think we can probably moor there after all!' So Biggles pushed on the joystick once more and this time the plane skated along the water. Just before he switched off the engine at the pier, he checked the fuel gauge. The pointer had dropped a little since his last look!

Move the pointer on your FUEL GAUGE one coloured segment clockwise. Now go to 230. (Remember: when the pointer reaches the DANGER segment on your FUEL GAUGE, you must immediately stop the game and start all over again from the beginning.)

As they were flying towards the wrecked ship, Biggles noticed that Bertie had a cigarette case in his hands. He tutted at him, reminding him that he was meant to have given up smoking. 'Oh, I have, old boy,' Bertie replied. 'Filthy habit! No, this is not *my* cigarette case – I found it down at the marsh. Look how tarnished it is. I'm looking to see if there's a name engraved on it, Wolff's for instance!' As Bertie examined the cigarette case further, he didn't manage to find Wolff's name but he *did* find what looked like some symbols of a code scratched on the outside!

Use your CODEBOOK CARD to find out what the symbols mean by decoding the instruction below. If you don't have a CODEBOOK CARD in your AIRCRAFT CARD, go to 38 instead.

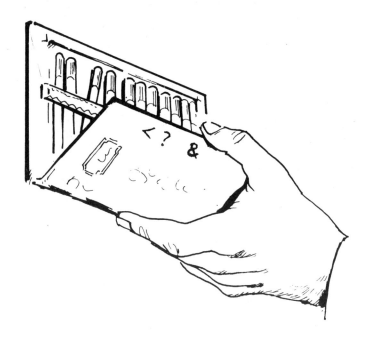

222

By the time Ginger had flattened the map on his knee, however, the waterfall was visible ahead of them. So he could now *see* how big it was . . . VERY! 'Gosh, look at all that spray rising from it,' he remarked as they flew nearer. 'That must be a good two hundred metres drop!' But Biggles was, for the moment, more concerned about another drop – the one showing on the plane's fuel gauge!

Move the pointer on your FUEL GAUGE one coloured segment clockwise. Now go to 153. (Remember: when the pointer reaches the DANGER segment on your FUEL GAUGE, you must immediately stop the game and start all over again from the beginning.)

223

Ginger reached the river-bank first, although the others were only a second or two behind! They now started to follow the river upstream, towards where they could hear the waterfall. Even from this distance it had quite a roar! They were still waiting for it to come into view, having trekked a good half-mile or so, when Bertie suddenly spotted a hunting knife lying on the muddy ground. 'It looks as if it's been here some time, judging by the rustiness,' he commented as he examined it. 'By Jove, look here, along the handle. Someone's scratched some symbols that look like a code!' He immediately reached into his pocket for his copy of Wolff's codebook . . .

Use your CODEBOOK CARD to find out what the symbols mean by decoding the instruction below. If you don't have a CODEBOOK CARD in your AIRCRAFT CARD, go to 273 instead.

224

Some forty minutes or so after landing on the lagoon, the trio reached the sorry collection of huts that constituted the village. It looked at first as if the whole place had been abandoned long ago but then they came across a solitary old man sheltering from the sun. He was puffing at a pipe, its stem held between toothless gums! *Go to 20.*

225

'Heavens above!' Bertie exclaimed as they finally approached the hut door again. 'Someone has wiped those chalked symbols off!' He turned, pale-faced, to Biggles. 'Maybe our aircraft being started up wasn't in your imagination after all, old chap. Perhaps it was a ploy simply to get us away from this door!' Just in case there *was* someone playing games with them, Biggles thought it best to return to their plane as quickly as possible. 'Phew, she's still here!' he said with relief some twenty minutes later. But as Biggles climbed into the Auster, he saw that his map was no longer on his seat. He could have sworn that he had left it there!

If you have it there, remove the MAP from your AIRCRAFT CARD. Now go to 106.

226

'Is that a piece of land there?' Biggles asked shortly after, peering into the blue-white haze on the horizon. 'Yes, I do believe it is! Unless we've got our bearings totally wrong, it looks as if we have found Flamingo Island!' As the mass of land came nearer, they all studied its coastline for some special feature that they could look for on their maps. This would confirm that it was Flamingo Island! 'How about that bottle-shaped islet on this side of the island?' Bertie suggested suddenly. 'Can you see it? It's about two miles out to sea. I know it's not very big . . . but probably just big enough to be shown on our maps!'

Do you have the MAP in your AIRCRAFT CARD? If so, use it to find which square the bottle-shaped islet is in – then follow the appropriate instruction. (Remember to return the MAP to your AIRCRAFT CARD afterwards.) If you don't have the map, you'll have to guess which instruction to follow.

If you think D4	go to 203
If you think D3	go to 280
If you think E4	go to 189

Biggles told Ginger that he was sure his compass wasn't necessary, though. 'Look, there's a rough track leading from the bay to the village,' he said as he now pushed on the control column to bring the Auster down. 'I'll try and get us as near to it as possible so there's no mistaking which way we have to go.' A quarter of an hour later the trio were following this rough track, Biggles very much hoping that the village would provide a vital lead. He had checked the plane's fuel level just before leaving the plane and was concerned to find it much lower than he expected!

Move the pointer on your FUEL GAUGE one coloured segment clockwise. Now go to 33.

The Auster now passed over the shore of Flamingo Island – at this part a stretch of rugged cliff. 'Look at those two massive caves down there,' Ginger said breathlessly. 'Now, if *I* was going to hide something, I'd give them serious thought!' So Biggles pushed on the control column, sending the Auster downwards so that they could have a better look at the caves. As he flew as close to the gaping entrances as he dared, they all searched for some possible evidence of Wolff's visit there!

Throw the SPECIAL DICE to determine who is to spot something.

BIGGLES thrown	go to 216
BERTIE thrown	go to 171
GINGER thrown	go to 69

229

'Just as I guessed!' Bertie exclaimed with delight when he had used his copy of Wolff's codebook to decode the symbols engraved on the watch. 'It works out as another name – that of our dear friend Werner! Christen Hagen is obviously just one of his many aliases.' So the team decided to make for the waterfall as quickly as possible and climbed back into the Auster. 'Much obliged to you!' Bertie shouted to the woman through his window as Biggles started the engine. *Go to 120.*

230

A few minutes later the team were hurrying along the river-bank, back towards the marsh. It certainly wasn't a very pleasant part of the island, with blood-sucking insects crawling in the under-growth. It was as they were ploughing through this infested undergrowth that Biggles suddenly tripped over something. 'Well

I never, it's a camera!' he exclaimed on picking it up. As Bertie took his turn to examine this curious find, he noticed what looked like the symbols of a code inscribed below the shutter. He quickly reached into his pocket for his copy of Wolff's codebook . . .

Use your CODEBOOK CARD to find out what the symbols mean by decoding the instruction below. If you don't have a CODEBOOK CARD in your AIRCRAFT CARD, go to 9 instead.

'Aren't you overlooking something, Ginger?' Biggles asked him as he eagerly took out his compass. 'That box might well have drifted since the message was scratched. So finding south-west could be misleading. No, I reckon our best bet is still that wreck out there!'
Go to 264.

232

Biggles and Bertie thought Ginger might well have a point. To reach the top of that mountain would no doubt involve quite a tough climb. This made it an ideal hiding place for the blueprints! So as the mountain came closer, Biggles looked for somewhere to land. 'Ah, just what I was hoping for,' he remarked on spotting a small lake beneath them. 'I would have preferred it a bit bigger but it should just about do!' It did very nicely, in fact, the Auster skiing to a neat halt just short of the lake's far end. The trio leapt out of the plane and prepared for their trek towards the mountain . . .

Throw the SPECIAL DICE to determine who is to lead on this journey.

BIGGLES thrown	go to 80
BERTIE thrown	go to 130
GINGER thrown	go to 192

233

As Bertie was taking out his codebook, however, the rotten plank suddenly gave way under his weight! Fortunately, he was quick-witted enough to jump clear or he might have fallen right through into the deep water below. 'Well, it's goodbye to that coded message!' Bertie remarked glumly, watching through the jagged hole as the broken plank fast disappeared. *Go to 243.*

'You're never going to believe this, you two!' Ginger exclaimed as they now approached the island's coastline. 'But I think it is a life-jacket that I've spotted!' Bertie thought this was just too much . . . until he also saw the brightly-coloured shape. It certainly seemed far too garish to be a boulder or anything like that. Whatever the thing was, it at least deserved a look through their binoculars!

Use your BINOCULARS CARD to obtain a clearer view of the orange shape by placing it exactly over the shape below – then follow the instruction. If you don't have a BINOCULARS CARD in your AIRCRAFT CARD, go to 170 instead.

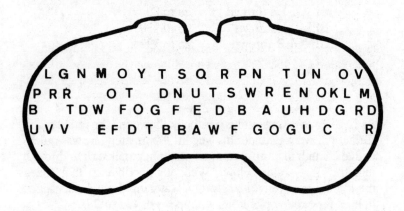

Ginger was far too restless to look for it on his map, though. He'd suddenly had an exciting thought. Maybe Wolff had used one of those kilns as his hiding-place! He was just going to suggest that they try and find somewhere to land when he noticed a couple of pigs near the entrance to one of the kilns. And trotting out of another were some goats! The island's inhabitants obviously used the derelict buildings to house their animals. So it wouldn't have been a very safe hiding-place for Wolff, after all! As the Auster now left the sugar plantation behind, Biggles glanced at the fuel gauge. The pointer had dropped once more!

Move the pointer on your FUEL GAUGE one coloured segment clockwise. Now go to 48.

236

The team had been in the air for half an hour or so since their last landing and were flying over the northern part of Flamingo Island, when Biggles spotted a number of ramshackle huts some way ahead of them. 'It's obviously a small village,' he said thoughtfully. 'I wonder if it's still inhabited? If it is, then maybe there's someone there who *saw* Wolff!' He asked if anyone could suggest a place to land so that they could go and investigate the village . . .

Throw the SPECIAL DICE to decide who is to make a suggestion.

BIGGLES thrown	go to 57
BERTIE thrown	go to 181
GINGER thrown	go to 117

237

When the woman saw Biggles produce his compass, however, she refused to let him read it! 'You don't need a fancy gadget to find the waterfall,' she told him. 'Just fly towards the sun!' Not wishing to offend the woman, Biggles put his compass away again. And to show their appreciation for her assistance, he asked Bertie to give the woman his pair of binoculars. They would help her keep an eye on those flamingos! 'With my compliments, madam,' Bertie said with a courteous bow as he handed over his binoculars.

If you have it there, remove the BINOCULARS CARD from your AIRCRAFT CARD. Now go to 210.

238

Bertie reached the Auster first and hauled himself in. A few seconds later Ginger took his seat as well – but they had to wait rather longer for Biggles. For some reason he had suddenly turned back to the boy. While they were waiting for him, Ginger thought he would see if this wrecked ship was shown on his map.

Use your MAP to find which square the wrecked ship is in – then follow the instruction. If you don't have a MAP in your AIRCRAFT CARD, you'll have to guess which instruction to follow.

If you think B1	go to 113
If you think A1	go to 185
If you think A2	go to 72

239

'Here's the house!' Ginger told the others when he had located it on his map. 'Apparently it was the residence of the island's governor. That explains that broken flagpole at the front. But I'm sure you're much more interested in how to find the waterfall from the house. Well, the answer is turn sharp right!' So Biggles immediately banked the plane to the right, rotating the control column. It was only a few minutes later that they spotted the waterfall, six or seven miles ahead of them. *Go to 153.*

'Do you think this is it at last?' Ginger asked excitedly as he laid the compass on the flat of his hand. 'Are the blueprints at the end of these seventy paces?' His excitement was so great that he had difficulty keeping his hand still and the compass needle was unable to settle. 'Here, let me have a go,' Biggles chuckled. 'There you are,' he added a few seconds later, pointing to their right. 'Due south is that way!' *Go to 202.*

Ginger reached the spot directly opposite the shipwreck first and stood squinting at it across the four hundred or so metres of water. It wasn't a very big ship – a two-mast schooner, as far as he could tell. While he was waiting for the others to join him, he thought he would see if the wreck was shown on his map. If it was, the *date* of the sinking might be given too . . .

Use your MAP to find which square the shipwreck is in – then follow the instruction. If you don't have a MAP in your AIRCRAFT CARD, you'll have to guess which instruction to follow.

If you think A4	go to 136
If you think A3	go to 52
If you think A2	go to 199

242

'Well?' Biggles asked impatiently as Bertie and Ginger studied the bright orange shape through their binoculars. 'Is it a life-jacket or isn't it? I can't keep circling round all day!' A moment later, though, Bertie was shaking his head in disappointment. 'I'm afraid it isn't, old chap,' he replied. 'It's just a mass of exotic-coloured seaweed that's been washed up. Not like seaweed that I've ever seen – but seaweed all the same!' *Go to 4.*

243

Their quick search of the harbour complete, Bertie and Ginger returned to Biggles at the Auster. As soon as they had climbed in, Biggles started up the plane's engine again, and the plane was soon skimming across the water. When they had lifted into the air, banking to the left to fly rather more inland, Ginger decided to look for the old harbour on his map. It would tell them precisely where they were on the island.

Use your MAP to find which square the harbour is in – then follow the instruction. If you don't have a MAP in your AIRCRAFT CARD, you'll have to guess which instruction to follow.

If you think D1	go to 129
If you think D2	go to 236
If you think C2	go to 152

244

'The mountain's height is given as just over a thousand metres,' Biggles informed the others after he had consulted his map. 'Well, I reckon we've already climbed at least seven hundred of those. So it shouldn't take that much longer to reach the top!' Ginger was just beginning to feel guilty that he might have led them all on a wild-goose chase when he spotted a compass on the ground. Although there was nothing to indicate that it had belonged to Wolff, it at least proved that *someone* had once been this way!

If you don't already have it there, put the COMPASS CARD into your AIRCRAFT CARD. Now go to 208.

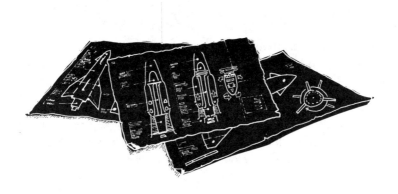

245

'HIDING-PLACE OF BLUEPRINTS IS VISIBLE FROM HERE!' Biggles announced excitedly, decoding the message that was carved into the wooden cross. But as he lifted his head to look round him, he saw that virtually the whole island was visible from that spot! 'It's obviously Wolff's idea of a joke!' Biggles remarked irritably as they now started the long climb down. 'We're no wiser than we were before!' ***Go to 194.***

246

The Auster ventured further and further inland, over more and more dense vegetation, but still the team couldn't spot anything that they might connect with Wolff. Suddenly, though, as they flew over a rare clearing, Bertie glimpsed a yellow bundle on the ground. 'By Jove, I think it might be a parachute!' he exclaimed. 'And if it is, there's surely a good chance that it might have been Wolff's! Who would want to parachute here, after all? But for Wolff, it would be the most discreet way he could arrive!' Before he became too excited about it, though, Bertie thought he'd better make absolutely sure it *was* a parachute. So he quickly started to unstrap his binoculars case!

Use your BINOCULARS CARD to obtain a clearer view of the bundle by placing it exactly over the shape below – then follow the instruction. If you don't have a BINOCULARS CARD in your AIRCRAFT CARD, go to 118 instead.

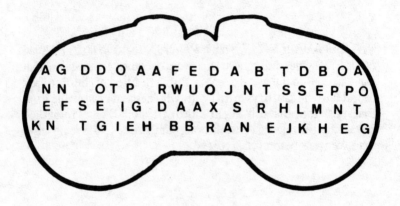

AG DDOAAFEDA B TDBOA
NN   OTP RWUOJNT SSEPPO
EFSE IG DAAX S R HLMNT
KN TGIEH BBRAN EJKHEG

247

'Where is this waterfall?' Bertie asked the woman keenly. But she was again reluctant to answer, not sure what to make of this strange man with a circle of glass in his eye! Ginger thought that he had better have a try. 'Perhaps you could point it out on my map?' he suggested amicably, reaching into his jacket pocket for it.

Use your MAP to find which square the waterfall is in – then follow the instruction. If you don't have a MAP in your AIRCRAFT CARD, you'll have to guess which instruction to follow.

If you think B2	go to 85
If you think A2	go to 260
If you think A3	go to 166

'Perhaps it's not in such bad condition after all,' Ginger remarked as he focused his binoculars on the little pier. 'Quite a few of the planks are broken but the supports look sturdy enough. It's probably as good a spot to aim for as any on that side of the river!' So Biggles immediately took the Auster down and sprayed to a halt just metres short of the little pier. **Go to 230.**

When Biggles heard Ginger unfolding his map behind him, however, he told him to put it away again! 'We can't have your head buried in that for the next few minutes,' he chuckled over his shoulder. 'We need every pair of eyes we've got looking out for this ship. It might be quite a small one – or very little of it sticking out of the water!' Biggles then turned his attention to Bertie, noticing that he no longer had his binoculars round his neck. He asked what had happened to them. 'Oh, nothing much,' Bertie replied rather coyly. 'I just thought that little chappie back at the marsh ought to have some sort of reward for all the help he gave us. The only thing I could think of was my binoculars!'

*If you have it there, remove the **BINOCULARS CARD** from your **AIRCRAFT CARD**. Now go to 145.*

'You won't need that,' the boy told Biggles when he saw him bring out his compass. 'I know about directions. My grandpa taught me. It's north-west for that evil ship.' So Biggles immediately put his compass away and thanked the boy again. 'It's north-west we have to fly!' he soon relayed to Ginger and Bertie as he took his place at the Auster's controls. *Go to 221.*

The bay proved to be far from the perfect landing site it had appeared. From above it looked completely clear of hazards but as the Auster skimmed along the surface of the water it suddenly jerked up into the air. They must have struck a rock! Fortunately, Biggles was able to keep the plane under control and finally brought it to a halt. And, fortunately too, the undercarriage had somehow escaped any damage. But the jolt had been so violent that Bertie's compass had jumped from his lap. Examining it, he found that the pointer no longer balanced properly!

If you have it there, remove the COMPASS CARD from your AIRCRAFT CARD. Now go to 201.

'South-west is out there!' Ginger exclaimed when he had consulted his compass. 'Exactly where that wreck is. So it looks as if our hunch was right. Wolff *did* choose it for his hiding-place!' Ginger was again about to let the box's lid drop shut when he stopped again. The box seemed to have a false bottom! He pulled out the thin sheet of metal that was wedged there and discovered a secret compartment. In it lay another of Wolff's codebooks!

If you don't already have it there, put the CODEBOOK CARD into your AIRCRAFT CARD. Now go to 264.

253

Ginger decoded the inscription as: *TOP SECRET BLUE-PRINTS CONTAINED INSIDE – FOR AUTHORISED EYES ONLY*. He immediately unscrewed the lid, believing it to be the end of their search, but he soon found the tube was empty! 'Don't look so down-hearted, Ginger,' Biggles consoled him. 'It doesn't necessarily mean that someone has got to the blueprints first, if that's what you're thinking. Wolff might have simply removed the blueprints from their container before hiding them. I still believe they're on that wreck!' Ginger was just about to give the tube an irritated kick when he noticed a pair of binoculars half-embedded in the ground nearby. Had these also been left by Wolff?

If you don't already have it there, put the BINOCULARS CARD into your AIRCRAFT CARD. Now go to 264.

254

Bertie waded to the bank first. When it came to facing a squadron of enemy aircraft, he was as brave as could be. But snakes . . . that was a totally different matter! They now started to follow the river-bank upstream, in the direction of the waterfall. They hadn't walked far, however, when they thought they heard a noise way above them. It sounded like a small aircraft or helicopter! 'I'll take a look through my binoculars,' Ginger said . . .

Use your BINOCULARS CARD to obtain a clearer view of the sky by placing it exactly over the shape below – then follow the instruction. If you don't have a BINOCULARS CARD in your AIRCRAFT CARD, go to 279 instead.

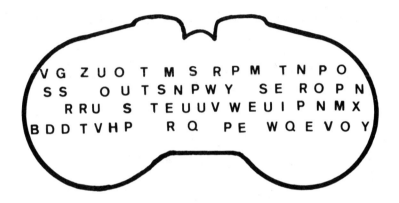

255

'I must have imagined it,' Ginger said as he focused his binoculars on the schooner. 'The deck's completely empty.' But as he put away his binoculars, he still felt rather uneasy. Maybe the boy had been right about the wreck being haunted! They hadn't rowed much further towards it when Biggles suddenly noticed a yellowing notebook under his seat. 'So this *was* the boat Wolff used to reach the wreck,' he announced on examining it. 'Look, this book has more of those codes of his!'

If you don't already have it there, put the CODEBOOK CARD into your AIRCRAFT CARD. Now go to 66.

'Well, what happens now?' Bertie asked wryly as the island came nearer and nearer. 'Finding the island is one thing, but finding the blueprints . . . that's a totally different kettle of fish! They could be absolutely anywhere!' Biggles couldn't help sharing Bertie's cynicism – it was going to be like looking for a needle in a haystack – but they had to give it a try. 'Let's land soon and get a feel of the place,' he said. 'You never know, we might be inspired! Anyone recommend where to put down?'

Throw the SPECIAL DICE to determine which of them is to suggest a landing spot.

BIGGLES thrown	go to 178
BERTIE thrown	go to 12
GINGER thrown	go to 77

'Sorry, old chap,' Bertie told Biggles as he focused his binoculars on the greyish hump. 'It *isn't* a boat! Well, you'd have trouble getting it to float anyway . . . it's actually a large boulder!' As Biggles now turned the Auster to the right, ready to start flying *across* the island, he gave a wry smile at his mistake. It just showed how desperate for a clue they were! ***Go to 158.***

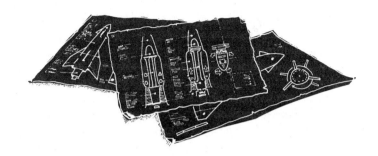

But Biggles immediately changed his mind about using his binoculars, and led the others in a fast scramble down the mountain. If there *was* someone snooping round their plane, it would probably make more sense to get back to it as quickly as possible! They took short cuts wherever they could, almost sliding down some of the slopes. At one point on the way down Biggles' map fell from his pocket but there wasn't even time to stop and pick it up!

If you have it there, remove the MAP from your AIRCRAFT CARD. Now go to 142.

'Look, that's a flock of flamingos, isn't it?' Biggles asked, suddenly pointing at a mass of specks in the distance. 'Yes, I'm sure it is! They could well be on their way back to the marsh. Let's try following them!' Bertie wasn't so certain about the birds being flamingos, though. Peering hard at them through his monocle, he thought that they were more likely to be geese! To save wasting fuel on what could literally be a wild-goose chase, he decided to get a better look through his binoculars . . .

Use your BINOCULARS CARD to obtain a clearer view of the birds by placing it exactly over the shape below – then follow the instruction. If you don't have a BINOCULARS CARD in your AIRCRAFT CARD, go to 209 instead.

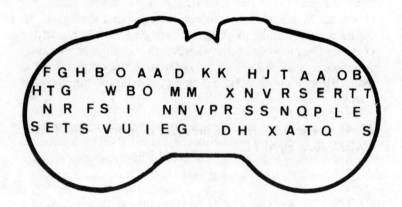

F G H B O A A D   K K   H J T A A   O B
H T G   W B O   M M   X N V R S E R T T
N R F S   I   N N V P R   S S   N Q P L E
S E T S   V U I E G   D H   X A T Q   S

'I don't need a map!' the woman said, with an arrogant toss of the head, just as Ginger was about to unfold it. She pointed a finger into the distance. 'The waterfall is over there,' she told them. 'You'll see it nice and clearly from your plane.' So the trio immediately climbed back into the Auster and Biggles steered it in the direction the woman had indicated. As they were flying, Ginger realised that he no longer had his compass in his pocket. He must have unknowingly pulled it out with his map!

If you have it there, remove the COMPASS CARD from your AIRCRAFT CARD. Now go to 197.

261
A few minutes later the Auster was touching down in the centre of the marsh after Biggles had decided that the water was just about deep enough. As the trio waded towards the edge, Bertie noticed a young teenage boy warily watching them from the reeds. 'Hello, old chap!' he called – but the boy immediately turned on his heels and ran. 'Hey, wait!' Bertie shouted, starting to give chase. 'We don't mean you any harm!' To begin with, Bertie didn't seem to have a hope of catching the boy, for he ran like a hare . . . but then the boy suddenly tripped and fell headlong on the soft ground. *Go to 28.*

262

'I can't see anything . . .' Ginger said, frowning, as he peered up through his binoculars. 'The trouble is that there's only a thin slice of the sky visible here anyway. All these dense trees have blocked most of it out.' So they still couldn't be sure whether there was a plane flying around up there or not! They were just about to continue their trek towards the waterfall when Biggles suddenly noticed a rusty compass on the ground. Could it have belonged to Wolff, he wondered!

If you don't already have it there, put the COMPASS CARD into your AIRCRAFT CARD. Now go to 89.

263

The team had only climbed a hundred metres or so down the mountain when Biggles suddenly tripped on a loose rock and fell forwards heavily! Fortunately, he didn't appear to have injured himself . . . but when he checked the binoculars that were hanging round his neck, he found that the lenses had shattered.

If you have it there, remove the BINOCULARS CARD from your AIRCRAFT CARD. Now go to 194.

The trio were just wondering how they were going to get over to the shipwreck – fearing the only way was to swim! – when Bertie noticed a small rowing-boat. It was half-hidden amongst the palm-trees just back from the beach. 'I wonder if this was the boat that Wolff himself used to reach the wreck?' Biggles asked as they all carried it to the water and jumped in. 'I can't see why else it would be sitting here!' As the wrecked schooner gradually came nearer, Ginger thought he saw someone on the deck. He nervously took out his binoculars!

Use your BINOCULARS CARD to obtain a clearer view of the ship's deck by placing it exactly over the shape below – then follow the instruction. If you don't have a BINOCULARS CARD in your AIRCRAFT CARD, go to 149 instead.

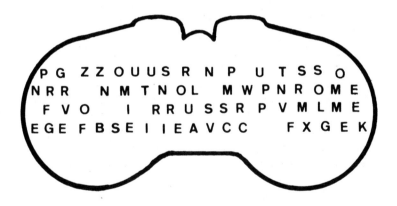

'My apologies, Ginger!' Bertie said as he looked through his binoculars at the place his young friend had been indicating. 'It would appear that Biggles and I *do* need our eyes testing after all. There *is* some land there!' So Biggles immediately turned the plane in this direction, pressing lightly on the right rudder pedal with his foot. It shouldn't be much longer now before they arrived at the island . . . *Go to 115.*

266

'Found her!' Ginger suddenly cried as he pointed his binoculars in the direction Biggles indicated. 'She's about a thousand metres above us. It's a light aircraft like ours, although I'm not sure what make. Hang on a minute – she's turning round, back towards Jamaica! It looks as if we don't have to worry about her after all!' But *was* she actually turning back towards Jamaica, Biggles wondered, or was it just a pretence, so they wouldn't be suspicious? *Go to 228.*

Ginger's compass showed that the palm-trees were leaning towards the west. It therefore seemed safe to assume that this was the direction of the prevailing wind. 'Well, let's hope we don't have too much trouble with the wind,' Biggles said over his shoulder as they continued on their course. 'I hear that it can sometimes reach hurricane force on these islands!' *Go to 173.*

Biggles was just opening his map, however, when he decided that perhaps it wasn't such a good thing for them to know the height of the mountain. Rather than encouraging them, it might *dis*courage them! So he returned the map to his jacket pocket but as he did so he noticed that his copy of Wolff's codebook was no longer there. The sheet of paper must have dropped out further down the mountain when, because it was so hot, he had taken off his jacket and slung it over his shoulder.

If you have it there, remove the CODEBOOK from your AIRCRAFT CARD. Now go to 208.

The dark foliage beneath them looked as if it would go on for ever but then it gave way to a vast area of a much lighter green. 'What sort of vegetation is that?' Ginger asked curiously. Biggles was asking himself the same question but then he spotted several derelict kilns amongst the yellowish-green. 'It's sugar-cane!' he suddenly realised. 'There was obviously some sort of plantation here many years go. See if it's marked on your map, will you, Ginger? It will tell us exactly where we are.'

Use your MAP to find which square the sugar plantation is in – then follow the instruction. If you don't have a MAP in your AIRCRAFT CARD, you'll have to guess which instruction to follow.

If you think D2	go to 235
If you think C2	go to 195
If you think B2	go to 48

270

As Ginger was opening his map, however, he was suddenly given a fierce jolt. The river wasn't the straightforward landing place it had appeared to be! 'We must have grazed a hidden rock!' Biggles said with alarm as he desperately tried to keep the Auster down on the water's surface. 'Let's hope there aren't any more of them!' Fortunately, there weren't and the plane skated to a more or less smooth halt. Biggles was just breathing a sigh of relief when he happened to glance at the fuel gauge. The pointer had dropped quite a bit since he'd last looked!

Move the pointer on your FUEL GAUGE one coloured segment clockwise. Now go to 164. (Remember: when the pointer reaches the DANGER segment on your FUEL GAUGE, you must immediately stop the game and start all over again from the beginning.)

Biggles reached the Auster first, just ahead of Ginger. But where was Bertie? Looking round to see what had happened to him, they saw that he had gone back to the boy! 'We forgot to ask him how to find the wrecked ship!' Bertie explained, some while later, when he had rejoined his two friends at the plane. 'Apparently, we're to follow the river down to the sea, then travel round the coast clockwise.' So Biggles immediately started following these directions, flying as low as possible. A short while after reaching the coastline, Ginger noticed a huge rock lying in a sandy bay. It was such a strange feature that he thought it might be shown on his map . . .

Use your MAP to find which square the rock is in – then follow the instruction. If you don't have a MAP in your AIRCRAFT CARD, you'll have to guess which instruction to follow.

If you think D4	go to 249
If you think C4	go to 145
If you think B4	go to 176

Ginger was still trying to find the large house on his map when at last Bertie spotted the waterfall. It was six or seven miles to their right. As Biggles now banked the plane in this direction, he happened to glance at the fuel gauge. The pointer had dropped quite a bit since his last look!

Move the pointer on your FUEL GAUGE one coloured segment clockwise. Now go to 153. (Remember: when the pointer reaches the DANGER segment on your FUEL GAUGE, you must immediately stop the game and start all over again from the beginning.)

273

'Ssh!' Biggles suddenly ordered just as Bertie was about to decode the symbols scratched on the knife. 'I thought I heard someone!' They all kept absolutely quiet, attentive to every tiny rustle of the leaves against the murmur of the river. 'I must have imagined it,' Biggles said after a couple of minutes. 'But just in case I didn't, I think we'd better try and get to the waterfall as quickly as possible. Bring that knife with you, Bertie. You can have another look at it later.' Biggles was in such a hurry to continue the rest of the journey that he didn't notice his compass lying on the ground. It had fallen out of his pocket when he had suddenly jerked to attention!

If you have it there, remove the COMPASS CARD from your AIRCRAFT CARD. Now go to 89.

'Leave your codebook for a moment, old boy!' Bertie told Ginger impatiently before he had a chance to take it out. 'Let's see what's inside the tube first!' So Ginger started to unscrew the lid, gritting his teeth with the effort because it had rusted on so tightly. At last it began to move. 'The tube's empty, I'm afraid,' he said disappointedly a few moments later. 'So I suppose there's no real point in decoding the inscription anyway. It presumably refers to what was once inside!' *Go to 264.*

The Auster circled over the bottle-shaped isle in the hope that the team might spot any clues that Wolff had left here as to the whereabouts of the blueprints. There seemed no particular reason why he should have done – but one never knew! 'Anyone see anything?' Biggles asked as he kept the plane at as low a height as possible.

Throw the SPECIAL DICE to determine who is to spot a possible clue.

BIGGLES thrown	go to 168
BERTIE thrown	go to 29
GINGER thrown	go to 151

As Ginger was opening out his map, though, Biggles suggested he wait until they found a rather less common geographical feature. 'For all we know,' he said, 'there could be a number of caves round this coast. How could you be sure you had located the right ones?' So Ginger folded up his map again and started looking out for a better landmark. But for the moment it was just mile upon mile of monotonous jungle. 'No wonder this place is so sparsely inhabited!' Biggles remarked as he glanced at the fuel gauge. The pointer had dropped a bit since he last looked!

Move the pointer on your FUEL GAUGE one coloured segment clockwise. Now go to 246.

Just as Biggles was about to swoop the Auster down towards the caves, however, he suddenly noticed a tidemark on them. It was a good three-quarters of the way up. In other words, they would be almost completely flooded when the tide was high! 'Wolff would have certainly noticed that as well,' Biggles pointed out to the others, 'and so he would surely have decided against using the caves as a possible hiding-place. Even if the blueprints had been put in a waterproof container, there would be a high risk of the sea dislodging them.' So Biggles pulled back on the control column, making the Auster climb up into the air again. As the plane started to fly across the island, over dense green vegetation, he took another look at the fuel gauge. The pointer had dropped a little since his last check.

Move the pointer on your FUEL GAUGE one coloured segment clockwise. Now go to 48.

278

Ginger was still focusing his binoculars on this dark patch of sea, however, when Bertie suddenly gave a cry of delight. 'Forget about down below, old boy!' he told him, wiping his monocle just to make sure what he had seen was real. '*There's* the shipwreck – about half a mile further along. You can see its whole front sticking out of the water!' So Biggles stopped circling the plane over this dark blue patch and immediately flew off towards the shipwreck. As he did so, he glanced at the fuel gauge. The pointer was lower than he would have liked!

Move the pointer on your FUEL GAUGE one coloured segment clockwise. Now go to 186. (Remember: when the pointer reaches the DANGER segment on your FUEL GAUGE, you must immediately stop the game and start all over again from the beginning.)

279

By the time Ginger had opened his binoculars case, however, the noise had gone. There was no point in looking any more! So he immediately strapped up his case again and the team continued on their way towards the waterfall. 'There's that noise again!' Bertie suddenly remarked a few minutes later. But Biggles told him that it was a totally different sound this time . . . the sound of tumbling water. The waterfall was obviously very close now! *Go to 89.*

280

'Are you sure we need consult a map?' Ginger asked, peering over Bertie's shoulder as his friend was reaching into his jacket pocket. 'If you remember, when we studied the charts back at HQ, there was only one island in this whole area west of Jamaica – Flamingo Island!' But Bertie told him he would like to make absolutely sure that was the case. 'Suppose this skipper of ours has been mistakenly flying east instead of west!' he said with a chuckle. *Go to 203.*

Having decoded the symbols on the plank, Bertie wiped his monocle thoughtfully. 'It works out as: *HEAD WEST ACROSS THE ISLAND*,' he informed Ginger as he carefully replaced the glass in his eye. 'But whether the author is our friend Wolff or not, it doesn't say!' While searching the rusty tin sheds just back from the pier, however, Ginger found the confirmation they wanted. In the corner of one of the huts was a pair of binoculars . . . and stamped across their front in small gold letters was the name *Werner Wolff*! 'He must have used these to keep a look out for anyone approaching the island,' Ginger speculated excitedly.

If you don't already have it there, put the BINOCULARS CARD into your AIRCRAFT CARD. Now go to 243.

No sooner had Biggles made the landing on the lake, stopping only metres from its shore, than the team splashed towards the rucksack. 'Drat, it's empty!' Bertie exclaimed as he tipped the red canvas bag upside down and gave it a shake. 'I was half hoping the blueprints would be inside!' As it was, there wasn't even any indication that the rucksack belonged to Wolff! Or was there? For Biggles suddenly noticed some faint ink-marks on the canvas. They looked like symbols of a code – and so he quickly reached into his pocket for his copy of Wolff's codebook!

Use your CODEBOOK CARD to find out what the symbols mean by decoding the instruction below. If you don't have a CODEBOOK CARD in your AIRCRAFT CARD, go to 59 instead.

283

They had still to reach the shore of Flamingo Island when Ginger suddenly spotted another aircraft in the sky – a red speck some distance to their right. Were they being followed? 'Try a little detour, skip,' he suggested, leaning right out of his window, 'and I'll see if the plane follows.' So Biggles banked sharply to the left, turning the Auster back towards the bottle-shaped isle. He continued right to its furthermost tip. As it turned out, the other plane *didn't* do the same – but the team still felt rather uneasy about it. Those extra miles had also caused a drop in their fuel!

Move the pointer on your FUEL GAUGE one coloured segment clockwise. Now go to 228.

284

Biggles circled round above the pattern of rocks as he waited for Ginger to produce his compass. Could this really be a clue from Wolff? If it was, it would certainly make their search a little easier! *Go to 2.*